VOICES F

Books by Louis Simpson

LOUIS SIMPSON

Voices in the Distance
SELECTED POEMS

BLOODAXE BOOKS

ISBN: 978 1 85224 861 1

First published 2010 by
Bloodaxe Books Ltd,
Highgreen,
Tarset,
Northumberland NE48 1RP.

www.bloodaxebooks.com
For further information about Bloodaxe titles
please visit our website or write to
the above address for a catalogue.

Supported by
**ARTS COUNCIL
ENGLAND**

Cover design: Neil Astley & Pamela Robertson-Pearce.

Printed in Great Britain by
Bell & Bain Limited, Glasgow, Scotland.

ACKNOWLEDGEMENTS

This book contains poems selected from Louis Simpson's *The Owner of the House: New Collected Poems 1940–2001* (BOA Editions, 2003) and *Struggling Times* (BOA Editions, 2009), with the exception of poems asterisked in the contents list, which are reprinted from his original American collections, *At the End of the Open Road* (Wesleyan University Press, 1963) and *Selected Poems* (Harcourt, Brace & World, 1965) and from *Collected Poems* (Paragon House, 1988).

The selection for this first UK *Selected Poems* by Louis Simpson since *People Live Here* (BOA Editions, USA, 1983; Secker & Warburg, UK, 1985) was made by Bloodaxe Books with the author's approval. Special thanks are due to David and Paulyn Church at Stony Brook, to Thom Ward and Nora A. Jones at BOA Editions, and to Richard Foerster, for their invaluable help and assistance with the work involved in publishing this book.

CONTENTS

Carentan O Carentan

Trees in the old days used to stand
And shape a shady lane
Where lovers wandered hand in hand
Who came from Carentan.

This was the shining green canal
Where we came two by two
Walking at combat-interval.
Such trees we never knew.

The day was early June, the ground
Was soft and bright with dew.
Far away the guns did sound,
But here the sky was blue.

The sky was blue, but there a smoke
Hung still above the sea
Where the ships together spoke
To towns we could not see.

Could you have seen us through a glass
You would have said a walk
Of farmers out to turn the grass,
Each with his own hay-fork.

The watchers in their leopard suits
Waited till it was time,
And aimed between the belt and boot
And let the barrel climb.

I must lie down at once, there is
A hammer at my knee.
And call it death or cowardice,
Don't count again on me.

Everything's all right, Mother,
Everyone gets the same
At one time or another.
It's all in the game.

I never strolled, nor ever shall,
Down such a leafy lane.
I never drank in a canal,
Nor ever shall again.

There is a whistling in the leaves
And it is not the wind,
The twigs are falling from the knives
That cut men to the ground.

Tell me, Master-Sergeant,
The way to turn and shoot.
But the Sergeant's silent
That taught me how to do it.

O Captain, show us quickly
Our place upon the map.
But the Captain's sickly
And taking a long nap.

Lieutenant, what's my duty,
My place in the platoon?
He too's a sleeping beauty,
Charmed by that strange tune.

Carentan O Carentan
Before we met with you
We never yet had lost a man
Or known what death could do.

The Man Who Married Magdalene

The man who married Magdalene
Had not forgiven her
God might pardon every sin...
Love is no pardoner.

Her hands were hollow, pale, and blue,
Her mouth like watered wine.
He watched to see if she were true
And waited for a sign.

It was old harlotry, he guessed,
That drained her strength away,
So gladly for the dark she dressed,
So sadly for the day.

Their quarrels made her dull and weak
And soon a man might fit
A penny in the hollow cheek
And never notice it.

At last, as they exhausted slept,
Death granted the divorce,
And nakedly the woman leapt
Upon that narrow horse.

But when he woke and woke alone
He wept and would deny
The loose behavior of the bone
And the immodest thigh.

The Battle

Helmet and rifle, pack and overcoat
Marched through a forest. Somewhere up ahead
Guns thudded. Like the circle of a throat
The night on every side was turning red.

They halted and they dug. They sank like moles
Into the clammy earth between the trees.
And soon the sentries, standing in their holes,
Felt the first snow. Their feet began to freeze.

At dawn the first shell landed with a crack.
Then shells and bullets swept the icy woods.
This lasted many days. The snow was black.
The corpses stiffened in their scarlet hoods.

Most clearly of that battle I remember
The tiredness in eyes, how hands looked thin
Around a cigarette, and the bright ember
Would pulse with all the life there was within.

I Dreamed That in a City Dark as Paris

I dreamed that in a city dark as Paris
I stood alone in a deserted square.
The night was trembling with a violet
Expectancy. At the far edge it moved
And rumbled; on that flickering horizon
The guns were pumping color in the sky.

There was the Front. But I was lonely here,
Left behind, abandoned by the army.
The empty city and the empty square
Was my inhabitation, my unrest.
The helmet with its vestige of a crest,
The rifle in my hands, long out of date,
The belt I wore, the trailing overcoat
And hobnail boots, were those of a *poilu*.
I was the man, as awkward as a bear.

Over the rooftops where cathedrals loomed
In speaking majesty, two aeroplanes
Forlorn as birds appeared. Then growing large,
The German *Taube* and the *Nieuport Scout*,
They chased each other tumbling through the sky,
Till one streamed down on fire to the earth.

These wars have been so great, they are forgotten
Like the Egyptian dynasts. My confrere
In whose thick boots I stood, were you amazed
To wander through my brain four decades later
As I have wandered in a dream through yours?

The violence of waking life disrupts
The order of our death. Strange dreams occur,
For dreams are licensed as they never were.

To the Western World

A siren sang, and Europe turned away
From the high castle and the shepherd's crook.
Three caravels went sailing to Cathay
On the strange ocean, and the captains shook
Their banners out across the Mexique Bay.

And in our early days we did the same.
Remembering our fathers in their wreck
We crossed the sea from Palos where they came
And saw, enormous to the little deck,
A shore in silence waiting for a name.

The treasures of Cathay were never found.
In this America, this wilderness
Where the axe echoes with a lonely sound,
The generations labor to possess
And grave by grave we civilise the ground.

The Runner

This is the story of a soldier of the 101st Airborne Division of the Army of the United States.

*   The Runner is fiction; the episodes and characters are imaginary. But the fiction is based on the following history.*

*   On September 7, 1944, parachute and glider infantry of the First British Airborne Division, the American 82nd and 101st Airborne Divisions, and a Polish brigade, descended in eastern Holland at Eindhoven, Grave, Nijmegen, and Arnhem. Their object was to make a bridgehead across the Lower Rhine at Arnhem. The British Second Army would join them and advance from Arnhem into the plains of northern Germany.*

*   At Arnhem the British airborne troops were attacked by enemy units in overwhelming strength and forced back across the river. The more fortunate Americans defended a corridor from Eindhoven to Nijmegen. The fighting, bitter at first, settled into a stalemate and, with the coming of the rainy season, petered out entirely.*

*   In mid-Novmber the 82nd and 101st were drawn back to Rheims, to re-equip and get the drizzle out of their bones.*

*   On December 17 they were alerted for combat. A German attack was developing in Belgium. The divisions were hurried by truck into the Ardennes, and on the night of December 19 the 101st were digging in around Bastogne.*

This poem is for Donald Hall who encouraged me to write it.

1

'And the condemned man ate a hearty meal,'
The runner said. He took his mess kit over
To the garbage can. He scraped his mess kit out,
Then dipped it in the can of soapy water,
And swished it in the can of clean, hot water,
And came back to his place.

                    The company
Was spread along one edge of the airfield,
Finishing lunch. Those with the appetite
Were going through the chow line once again.
They looked all pockets, pockets and baggy pants.
They held their mess kits out to the sweating cooks,

Who filled them up, then bore their precious load
Apart.

      The runner felt in his breast pocket
For cigarettes. He lit one and inhaled.
Leaning back on his pack, his feet sprawled out,
He stared at the ranks of gliders and towplanes
And said, 'I wonder if...'

                'Agh!' said a voice,

'Why don't you dry up, Dodd!'

He looked around
And met the eyes of Kass, the radioman,
Glaring beneath the rim of his steel helmet.

'What?' said the runner.

           'Who needs your remarks?
First, the condemned men eat a hearty meal,
And then you wonder...'

           'When we're coming back.'
'What's it to you?'

      The runner didn't answer.
Sometimes it seemed that anything he said
Rubbed someone the wrong way. He'd only meant
He hoped the outfit would come back to England
And London, where he'd gone on two-day passes.
He liked the pubs, the mugs of mild-and-bitter,
And country lanes. Some day, when they came back
He'd go off on his own. Rent a bicycle.
He'd see some of the country by himself.
And if he got to London...

      With a roar
An engine started. Other engines followed.
A gale from the propellers swept around him.

'Fall in!' said the First Sergeant.

                         Dodd got up
And hoisted on his pack.

                    'Get a move on!'

That's how it was: you always had to wait,
And then you had to hurry. He closed his belt,
And slung his rifle over his right shoulder.
The section formed.

                    'Where's Wheeler?' said the sergeant.
And here came Wheeler at a run. 'You, Wheeler...'
The sergeant followed him with imprecations
As Wheeler ducked in place at Dodd's right hand.
Out of the side of his mouth: 'Look what I got,'
Said Wheeler, and he showed in his clenched fist
A bundle of the new invasion money.
'Over in F Company,' he whispered.
'The dice was really hot.'

                    'Ten-*hut!* For-*ard
Arch!*' said the sergeant, and they started off
Across the concrete runway. It seemed long.
Dodd's mouth was dry; his legs were weak. At last
They came up to the glider, their box kite –

High wings and rudder, little wheels that hardly
Lifted it off the ground – a canvas coffin.
Ungainly as a duck, it wouldn't fly
Unless it had to.

                    Through the open door
Under the wing they climbed up one by one,
Toppling with their burdens. Found their seats.
And sat in two rows, looking at each other.
Dodd fastened his safety belt and clasped his gun
Between his knees. The Captain entered last.
They waited. The glider trembled in the blast
Of wind from the towplane. The pilots entered,
Leaping up lightly, and made their way forward
To the controls.
                    The runner could see nothing

Beyond the glider's high, transparent nose;
But now, he thought, the towplane would be turning
Into the wind. Two men would run the cable
Back from the plane and hook it to the glider.
Then, with a louder blast of the propellers,
The plane would start to roll.

                       The glider jerked
Forward, and rolled, creaking, and gathered speed.
The bumping stopped, and with a sudden lightness
They were airborne. Constricted where he sat,
Dodd prayed to nothing in particular:
Let the rope hold; no current whirl us down
Smashing on concrete.

                    They were well away.
He stared at the slender pilots in their pinks
And sporty caps and glasses; at their hands
On the half-wheel. His life was in those hands.
He thought of shell bursts, the green canvas torn,
Men writhing in their belts, the pilots' hands
Fallen from the controls, a sickening drop.
And then he thought of fields with pointed stakes
That would shear through the sides. Of plunging out
Into machine-gun fire.

    2

                  'We're almost there,'
The next man said.

                  The pilots were peering down.
One nodded, and the other raised his hand
And grasped the lever that released the cable,
And pulled it down.

                 The glider soared, then fell
Slanting away. The wing rose up again.
They glided down on silence and the wind.

The fields were rushing at them, tilted steep.
Dodd braced himself. The glider leveled, lightly
Bumped on the ground, and rolled to a dead stop.

The door was open. They were climbing through.
And now were standing in an open field
Flat as a pancake. Gliders strewed the scene.
Others were skimming down; and still the sky
Was filled with gliders.

From their lifted bows
The gliders were disgorging jeeps and cannon.
Riflemen formed their files and marched away.
Dodd's section took its place in the company.
The Captain raised his arm; he swept it down,
And they were marching.

On the bright horizon
A windmill stood. The land was crossed with dykes.
It looked like a Dutch painting. To their left
A wood began. They marched in that direction.

The day was hot, and Dodd began to sweat.
Then to his ears came the familiar sound
Of guns, the battle-roll, continuous.
Then all his other days were like a dream.
This was reality: the heat, the load
Strapping his shoulder, and the sound of guns.
The war, after Normandy, had seemed remote.
He had been there; his courage had been proved
To his own satisfaction. He had listened
To talk about the fighting, and he'd talked
And lost the sense of truth. He had forgotten
The smell of apples and the fear of death.
Now he remembered. And it seemed unjust
That he should be required to survive
Again. The sound increased. The battleground
Looked ominous. Visions of a huge mistake
Struck at his heart.

3

The company was entering the woods.
'Dodd,' said the sergeant, 'take this message up
To Lieutenant Farr.'
He stepped out of the file
And hastened to the front. The lead platoon

Was walking slowly, with the scouts ahead.
He gave the message.

     'Right,' said the lieutenant.
The runner started back. As he went by
Faces stared into his inquiringly.
He seemed possessed of an important secret.

Shots went off behind him. He crouched and swung
Out of the path, and lay in the scrub, face down.
The firing stopped. A voice was calling 'Medic!'

Fisher, a sergeant of the third platoon,
Came up the path, bent low. He shook Dodd's shoulder:
'Who's doing all the shooting?'

     '*I* don't know,'
Dodd said. The sergeant, with a grim expression,
Stared at him, and went on.

     The runner waited.
Why didn't they get it over with!

     'Move out!'

He got to his feet. The path filled up with men.
He made his way back, past the sweating faces
Now streaked with dust. He fell in with his section,
Turned round, and traveled up the path again
He'd just traversed.

     The files ahead were parting.
The men looked down, as into a precipice.
There was a body lying in the way.
It was Santelli, of the first platoon.
Dodd had just seen him going out in front;
He walked like a dancer, with a short, neat step,
Rifle held crosswise.

     He lay huddled up
On his left side; his helmet had rolled off;
His head was seeping blood out in the dirt.

The files ahead were lagging; then they hurried.
'Keep your intervals!' the Captain shouted.
They hated him together.

             At the break
They sprawled out of the path, in the underbrush.
Santelli's death had made them strangely silent.
Their helmets bowed their heads down on their chests.
Under the distant thudding of the guns,
The weight of all their burdens and the sky,
They couldn't speak, or stir themselves, or lift
A cigarette.

             Dodd thought about Santelli.
One of the afternoons it seemed forever
All they would do was practice for the war
With marches, tactics, and map exercises,
He lay beneath the wall of an English garden,
Sucking a stalk of grass, and watched the clouds,
And far above the clouds, a fleet of bombers
Trailing long plumes of white across the blue.
Close by, Santelli sat, paring his nails
With a pocketknife.

                'Hey, runner-boy,' he said
In the familiar and sneering tone
That Dodd despised. 'What're we doin, hey?
You've been to college, right?' His little eyes
Were sharp with mockery – a little man
Of pocketknives and combs. 'You ought to know.
What's it all about?'

    4
A plane flew glittering out of the sun –
A *Thunderbolt*. It swooped and disappeared
Behind a screen of trees. Then a staccato
Sound began. Machine guns. The plane rose
And flew away. They watched it till it vanished.

'On your feet,' the sergeant said.

                'My aching back!'

Someone said; but the gripe lacked conviction.
They stood and crumbled out their cigarettes,
And rolled the paper into little balls,
As though they'd like to keep the battlefield
Clean as a barracks.

As Dodd marched, the weight
Sawed at his shoulders: pack and ammunition,
Gas mask and trench tool, bayonet, grenades.
He plodded with clenched jaws, his eyes cast down
On the dusty path, the heels moving ahead.
He stayed, it seemed, in a fixed position;
It was the scene that moved.

The path reeled in
Another corpse. It came to him boot-first:
A German soldier on his back, spread-eagle,
A big, fresh-blooded, blond, jack-booted man
In dusty gray. Stepping around the fingers,
Around the bucket helmet, Dodd stared down.
A fly lit on the teeth. He looked away
And to the front, where other attitudes
Of death were waiting. He assumed them all,
One by one, in his imagination,
In order to prevent them.

Small-arms fire
Was crackling through the wood. Platoons spread out
In arrow-shaped formations.

'Dig in!'

He dug.
The shovel sank in sand; he hacked at roots.
Overhead, shells were whispering, and smoke
Came drifting back.

Two planes went whistling over.
Typhoons. They darted searching on the front.
They dived, and from their wings plunged rockets down
In smoking streaks. The ground shook with concussions.

'We're moving out!'

                              Dodd climbed out of the hole
That he had dug. The company moved in silence
Through the burning wood.

    5

Beyond the wood there stretched an open road.
They filed out on it. In a field of hay
A plane perched on its nose, a *Messerschmidt*,
The black cross glaring.

                        Houses stood here and there.
In front of one, a mattress had been laid,
And on the mattress, a German officer.
He was puffed up with air like a balloon,
Belly and limbs swelling as if to split
His uniform. The grass was stuck with feathers.

Night was falling; the light had left the fields.
The road approached a village. At the entrance
A German half-track had been blown apart,
Its mustard-yellow metal torn and scorched;
Out of it spilled the crew, burned black as rubber.
The street, as they passed through, was strewn with dead,
A presentation of boot soles and teeth,
Letters, cigars, the contents of their lives.

The cannonading was more loud, and flashes
Lit the darkening sky. A company
Of paratroopers passed them, coming back
With somber faces.

    6

Night. And the fields were still. The cannonade
Was flickering and grumbling through the sky.
Red flashes lined the clouds. No breath of wind
Was moving. In the holes that they had dug
The tired troops were sleeping on their arms.

'Dodd, get up!'

                        He struggled out of his bag.

The First Sergeant leaned over: 'Take this message
Back to Battalion.'
Dodd took the paper,
His helmet and his M-1, and set off,
Still half asleep.

              Darkness without a moon
Surrounded him. He made his lonely way
Over a road that skirted trees and dykes.
The guns were rumbling; shells went fluttering over;
Machine-gun tracers sparkled distantly.
A flare popped in the sky and glimmered down;
He waited in the shadow of a tree
Till it went out. And took the road again.
A deepening of black, a looming wall,
Was Battalion C.P. The guard called out:
'Halt! Who's there?'

              The runner spoke the password:
'Kansas!' and was admitted by the guard
Into the courtyard. There he gave his message
To a tech-sergeant; sat down on a bench,
And waited, looking at the pulsing sky.

'Runner!'

      He answered.

              'Take this message back.'
That was his job. Now all I need, he thought,
Is one of those Philip Morris uniforms
The bellboys wear.

              The road was long and dark.
And it was weird to be alone in Holland
At midnight on this road. As he went on
He felt he had no weight. The landscape seemed
To have more things to think of than his journey.
These errands gave him little satisfaction.
Some men might think he led the life of Riley,
Safe and warm and dry, around Headquarters.
A man could be a runner all his life

And never be shot at. That's what they thought.
But how about the shelling? He'd been shelled
As much as anyone. And back in France,
At Carentan, he had been shot at – plenty!
It wasn't his fault he never had a chance
To fire back. Now right here on this road,
He might be killed by accident. But still,
That wouldn't be the same as being brave.
He had no chance to be thought so, no part
In the society of riflemen.
So, as he went, he reasoned with himself.

    7

Next day the company went up on line
Near Veghel. They were digging round a church,
In the cemetery, and were just knee-deep
When hell broke loose.

                The screaming and flat crack
Of eighty-eights.

        Airbursts.

                The metal slashed
The trees and ricocheted. Bit in the ground.

The runner on his belly lay contracting
Under the edge of metal. From a tree
A yard away, leaves flew. A voice cried 'Medic!'

His belly and his buttocks clenched each time
A shell came in. And they kept coming in.
He felt a sting between his shoulder blades.
I'm wounded, he thought, with a rush of joy.

'Dodd!' someone called.

             He went on hands and knees
Toward the voice. 'Over here,' it urged him.
It was his sergeant, with a dozen cases
Of mortar shells.

'Take them up to the mortars,'
he said. 'They're out of ammunition.'

He took two cases, one beneath each arm,
And ran off, dodging among the trees and graves.
He found the mortars and came running back
To get another load. The crack and hum
Of the artillery was all around him.
He felt the sting of the place where he'd been hit.
He knew that he was brave.

On the last trip,
Kneeling above a mortar, as he lowered
The cases gently, one of the mortar crew
Said, 'You're a good man, Dodd.'

That night he lay
Smiling, without a care, beneath the sky.
He had done all that could be expected.

8

October, and the sky was turning gray.
The battle line had settled. Every night
The bombers flew, going to Germany
At a great height. And back the other way
The V-1's came. The soldiers in their holes
Heard them droning and saw the rhythmic flames
Carrying woe to Antwerp and to England.

They dozed or watched. Then it began to rain,
And always rained. It seemed they were never dry.
Winter was in the air. Paths turned to mud.
By day and night the shells came shrieking in;
They got so they could tell a dying fall
And pay the rest no mind. They lived with mud.
They cooked and ate their rations in the can,
And tried to dry their socks between two rains.
Cold and sullen, under a raincoat roof,
They shivered in their holes.

One moonlit night
Dodd was returning on his way alone.

There was a wind; the haunted shadows stirred,
And rainpools glimmered in the moonlit fields.

There was a field the runner loathed to cross.
A place of horrors. Here, on the first day,
There'd been fierce charges, combats at close range,
And the dead were mixed as they had fallen.
Here crouched the German soldier with his *schmeisser*
Close to the parachutist in his rage –
Putrid things, never to be forgotten.
The field was swelling, shining with an aura
Of pale corruption.

       To avoid it, Dodd
Went by another path he did not know,
Leading, it seemed, back to the company.
But in a while a fearful premonition
Stopped him. In a shadow, cold with dread,
He stood listening. The branches stirred,
And all at once there was a clash of arms,
The sounds of footsteps. Stealthily he turned
To slip away.

     'Wer geht da?'

       He ran.
He plunged into the darkness, blind with panic.
A storm of shots erupted at his back.
Brambles tore at his legs. He climbed a bank,
Clawing, and stumbled down the other side.
Then, as he ran, he shouted out the password.
'Ohio!' like a dog drenched with hot water.
His rifle fell. He left it where it was.
'Ohio!' He collided with a branch
And staggered. At his back the storm increased.
Red tracers streaked the air. Across a ditch
He leaped. And ran across the road beyond.
A hole was in his way; he cleared it with
A stride, and the dark figure starting up
Out of the hole. He kept on running, shouting
'Ohio!' A shape standing in the path
Snatched at him; he swerved out of its grasp.

There was a maze of holes. He stumbled, reeled,
And fell. His helmet flew off with a clang.

Feet were approaching. He lay still as death.
'It's Dodd,' said a voice.

                    At last, he looked up
Into the faces of the third platoon.
Fisher. Others. They looked down in wonder.

   9

The regiment was bivouacked near Rheims
In tents on the bare plain. Wind-driven clouds
Streamed over, and the land in chilly streaks
Heaved like a sea. The wind hummed on the ropes
And whipped the tent flaps.

                    Dodd, stretched on his cot,
Could see and hear the third platoon at drill.
They turned to the flank and to the flank again;
They marched to the rear.

                    'Count cadence...cadence count!'
'*Hup*...two...three...four!' they answered on the wind.
The sun flashed from the slanting rifle butts.
The corporal shouted: 'When I say Ohio,
To the rear march, and double-time like hell!'
There was a burst of laughter, then: 'Ohio!
Run!' the corporal said, '*Hup*...two...three...four!
Halt! Now we'll try that movement once again.
When I give the word Ohio, turn around
And double-time as if your name is Dodd.
Make it look good. All right now – forward 'arch!
Ohio!'

    Dodd rolled over on his face.
He saw himself once more before the Captain:
'Screaming the password...throwing away your gun...
Keep out of my sight, Dodd. You make me sick.'

And then, the jokes, from reveille to sleep:
'That is Ohio, one of the midwest boys.'

Replacements would be sent to see Ohio
To draw their running shoes. 'I'm from Cleveland,'
One of them told him. 'What part are you from?'

He turned upon his back. Right overhead
His jacket hung, with regimental ribbons,
The bronze star, and his shameful purple heart.
He stared at it. If he could only sleep
The time between, until the sergeant came
To put him on another hard detail!

That was his punishment: to dig latrines,
Pick cigarette butts up, scrub greasy pots –
Or to do nothing for a live-long day
But think and try to read, in a cold tent.

When the men came in, they would ignore him –
'You going in to town?'
                                      'You said it, man!'

Polishing up their paratrooper boots
Until the toes reflected a lit match;
Blousing the trousers in their boot tops; brushing
Their jackets; tucking ties between two buttons;
Cocking their caps – 'Let's go!'

                                      He fell asleep,
And dreamed that he was climbing. On the crest
A dummy stood, with stiff, ballooning arms
And painted face, in Prussian uniform.
He reached the arms and swung them. It went 'B-r-r-r-m!'
Like a machine gun. 'B-r-r-r-m!' the sound came out
The dummy's painted lips and barrel belly.
Then he was walking over a green field.
It was a country he had never seen,
With haystacks, a warm wind, and distant barns.
Shadows were walking with him, and a voice
Spoke with the measure of a travelogue:
'*Vingtième Division*…fifty per cent…'
Another voice inquired: 'Casualties?'
'No,' said the first voice, 'all of them are dead.'
And it continued: '*Douzième Infanterie*…

Fifty per cent...' As the first voice was speaking,
Over the field, as on a movie screen,
Hands were imposed; they held a scarlet cloth
And folded it. 'René de Gaumartin,'
The voice continued, 'Cardinal of France.'
Again the hands were folding a red robe.
'Marcel Gaumartin, Cardinal of France.'
And as the voice and the pale hands continued
Their meditative play, Dodd came upon
A girl in black. She had fair hair and skin,
Plain features, almost ugly, but her eyes
Were large, they shot out tender rays of light.
The voice said, 'Mademoiselle de Maintenon.'
In his dream, Dodd laughed. *De Maintenon!* She said,
In a voice remote with sadness, 'Yes,' and smiled,
'I try not to think of them too much.'

                                    He woke,
And his heart was light. It was a vision,
He thought. What does it mean? What eyes she had!
That field, with the wind blowing, and the clouds!
And yet, it was absurd. The words were nonsense.

He went out of his tent.

                        The third platoon
Were sitting down, taking a smoking break.
'Ohio!' someone shouted. 'Where you running?'

He walked the other way, toward a rise
With trees, the only trees in all the plain,
Leaving the tents behind.

                        He climbed the slope
And sat beneath a tree. On the horizon
Rheims, with the cathedral, like a ship
Traveled the plain. Clouds were streaming over
The spire; their swift shadows ran like waves.
He lit a cigarette. Then, near at hand,
He saw the earth was trenched. A long depression,
No more than a foot deep, with rotten posts
And scraps of wire, wound across the slope.

He stood, and walked along it. The earth gave
Under his boots. He picked up a small scrap
Of wire, and it crumbled. He surmised
This was a trench dug in the first Great War.
Who knew? Perhaps an older war than that.
He faced the East, to Germany and Russia.
Shadows were standing with him. It was cold.

They watched, wrapped in old overcoats, forgotten.
They stamped their feet. The whole world was deserted
Except for them; there was nobody left.
On the imagined parapet, a cross
Howled in the wind; and there were photographs
Of girls and children, bunches of cut flowers.

Then, on the pitted, gaunt escarp, the night,
The melancholy night, swept with grandeur.
Far in the dark, star shells were blossoming.
They stamped their feet. It was too cold. Too much
To expect of them. Their boots sank in the mud.
Their veins seemed ice; their jaws creaked with the cold.
They spoke; their words were carried on the wind,
Mingled, and lost.

                But now, an actual sound
Arrived distinctly. When he turned to look,
The camp was stirring; men ran to and fro.
He saw the third platoon halt in their drill,
Fall out, and run toward their tents. He moved;
He ground his cigarette out underfoot,
And hastened down the slope.

                     'Where have you been?'
Said the First Sergeant.
                 'I've been for a walk.
What's going on?'
                'Full field. Ready to move
In half an hour.'

            Dodd's tent was in confusion.
The men were cramming rations in their packs,
Rolling their sleeping bags, cleaning their weapons.

He labored with stiff fingers.

                          Trucks drew up
Outside.

        'Get a move on!' a corporal shouted.

Dodd hitched on his pack.

                    The company
Fell in and shuffled, straightening their ranks,
Eyes to the right.

          'Let's go!'

                    Dodd took his place
In the line of olive drab, the overcoats,
Helmets, packs, the gloved hands holding weapons.
The roll was called; he answered to his name.

They marched up to the trucks.

                    'Mount up!'

                              He climbed
Into the truck, and was packed in. The gate
Clanged shut behind him.

    10

Day turned to dusk; the truck went jolting on;
The wind was drumming on the canvas hood
And prying coldly down the runner's back.
Dusk turned to evening, and the trucks behind
Were hidden. He dozed off. Monotony
Had numbed his senses like an anesthetic.
When the gears shifted he would nearly wake.
Sometimes the truck would stop for no clear reason,
And faces, blinking in their woolen caps,
Lifted and muttered; someone tried to stretch,
And this set off a ripple of complaints.
Then the truck moved again.

Once they dismounted,
And Dodd saw that the road wound through a forest.
There was a hill on one side; on the other,
The trees descended into a ravine.
Against that bank, a group of people stood:
Women and children dressed in country black,
With kerchiefs round their heads, and an old man
Close by a cart. The cart was piled with things:
A mattress, pots and pans. They stood in silence
Watching the soldiers. Then the trucks reloaded,
And the onlookers vanished.

                    They were driving
More slowly now. The men were all awake.
Another stop. Again the tailgate opened,
And they dismounted.

                 This, then, was the place.
Colliding in the dark, they formed platoons,
And marched away.

               A signpost read *Bastogne*.
They marched through a dark village with locked doors,
And were led off the road, into the woods.
The path was very dark, the march confused,
With frequent halts.

             They halted in one place
Endlessly; they reclined, propped on their packs.
His helmet dragged Dodd's head back on his neck;
His feet got cold; under his woolen shirt
The sweat was trickling, then began to chill.

Then they were roused, pressed on without a pause,
Till, on a ridge commanding a black slope,
They halted. And the order came: 'Dig in!'

Dodd unhitched his pack, laid it on the ground,
And leaned his rifle on it. From his belt
He took his trench tool out, and opened it.
He stuck the shovel blade into the ground
And levered it. He'd barely circumscribed

35

A foxhole, when a cold chill touched his cheek –
Snow!

      That's all we needed, the runner said
To the malignant sky.

          From branch to branch
Snow glimmered down and speckled the dim ground.
Dodd dragged a fallen branch across his hole
And made a roof.

        'Pack up,' the sergeant said.
'We're moving out.'

        God help them, they were led
By officers and morons, who had orders
For wearing leather out and breaking spades,
To give employment to the men at home
Who, on this freezing night, were warm in bed
With soldiers' wives!

        Having said so, they walked
On in the stumbling dark, till once again
They halted, in a place just like the first.

'Dig in!'

      And it was useless, but they dug
With the energy of a supreme contempt
Marvelous holes – each clammy wedge of earth
An accusation flung in heaven's face.

Then, like a sound engendered by their mood,
An angry muttering rose on the night.
It faded, and again came to their ears –
The sound of guns.

       At last, Dodd's hole was finished.
He lowered himself, rolled out his sleeping bag,
And pushed into it. Flickerings of light
Twitched overhead; the guns were coming closer.
Here, it was still. The snow came drifting down.

'Dodd, you're on guard.'

      He climbed out of his hole.

'There, by the trees.'

     He walked across the snow,
And as he went he looked around, astonished –
The sky was lit with spots of burning red
In a great circle.

    As he stood on guard,
Surveying the black slope, the distant fires,
A man approached. Dodd challenged him. He spoke
The password, and came slogging through the trees.
A runner from Battalion. Brushing snow
Out of his neck, he asked for the C.P.
Dodd pointed: 'Over there. Close to the barn.
What's happening now?'

     'We're up a creek, that's what!
They're coming – panzers from the Russians front,

Under Von Runstedt. Panzers and SS.
I was just talking to a man who said
The line at St Vith has been overrun
By tanks. It was a total massacre.
They're dropping paratroopers too,' he said,
And turned away. He paused again to add:
'Everyone else is pulling out but us,'
And trudged away, leaving Dodd to his thoughts.

 11

The night was long. And day seemed less to rise
Than darkness to withdraw. Dodd, in his hole,
Could hear the fire of small arms, that seems
More threatening to the solitary man
Than does artillery.

    One hole away
A helmet like a turtle shell was stirring.
A puffy face with whiskers turned around;

It was the mailman, Lopez. He arranged
Twigs on the snow. On these, his drinking mug.
He struck a match, applied it to the twigs,
And nursed the flame with cupped hands, bending over.

Under the hanging sky, congealed with clouds,
Fog trailed and clung to the earth; and the Ardennes,
The spectral firs, their branches cloaked with snow,
Stood stark against the foggy atmosphere.

Dodd stamped his feet. He stooped, and from his pack
Took a K-ration box. He tore it open,
Shook out the can of egg, the pack of biscuits,
The packet of coffee. He removed a glove
And with that hand put snow into his mug.
Poured coffee in, and mixed it with his spoon.
He scooped a hollow in the snow, and piled
Some twigs in it, and strips of the ration box.
And then put the mug on, and lit the pile.

Voices came floating up – loud gutturals;
A whine and clanking of machinery.
He picked his gun up.

                        At the foot of the slope
The trees were shaking, parting. There emerged
A cannon barrel with a muzzle brake.
It slid out like a snake's head, slowly swinging.
It paused. A flash of light came from its head;
A thunder clap exploded to Dodd's left;
Metal whanged on the slope, a spume of black
Hung in the air.

                        Then, endlessly it seemed,
The barrel slid out. With a thrash of branches
A tank appeared. It lurched, seemed to consider,
And then came on, at an appalling rate.
The engine whined; the tracks jingled and squeaked.
And imperceptibly, out of the trees
Stood men, like apparitions of the snow.

And now it was a swarm of walking men
In field-gray and in white, with capes and hoods.

Dodd placed his elbows on the snow, took aim –
There was another thunder clap. He ducked
And came upright again. To left and right
Rifles were firing. Hastily he pointed
The muzzle at a running, hooded shape,
And pressed the trigger. As in a nightmare
Nothing happened. A bullet cracked by his head.
The safety catch was on. He pressed it – forward,
And aimed the gun again, and squeezed the trigger.
The butt kicked in his shoulder, the brass jumped
Into the snow.

       The tank was growing large.
The cannon flashed. Machine-gun tracers curved
Toward it, and played sparkling on the steel.
Still it came on, glittering in return
From its machine guns. Then, a crashing flame
Struck it, leaving a trail of smoke in air.
The tank shuddered. It slewed broadside around.
Inside the plates, as on an anvil, hammers
Were laboring. It trembled with explosions,
And smoke poured out of it.

          The slope was still,
Sprawling with hooded figures – and the rest
Gone back into the trees. Then there began
The sound of the wounded.

        Dodd stood up
And looked around. In the next hole, a helmet
Moved cautiously.

     'Lopez,' he inquired,
'Are you all right?'

     'Jesus!' the mailman said.
With a shaking hand, Dodd felt for cigarettes.
He breathed tobacco deep into his lungs.
On the twigs where he had left it balanced
His mug was hissing and – he held it – warm.

Sometimes the snow came drifting down again.
And when it ceased, eddies and gusts of wind
Would lift it in long skirts that swept across
The dead. It packed into the stiffened folds
Of clothing. When night fell, a freezing wind
Encased the tree trunks in bright sheaths of ice
And hung bright icicles on every branch,
And clamped the dead in rigid attitudes.

A shell came whistling down. The runner clenched
His fists. It crashed. Another shell came in.
The crashes jarred the ground. Then, from the rear,
A battery replied; shells fluttered back.

'Dodd!'

   He unzipped his bag, put on his helmet,
And stood.

    'Where are you?'

      It was the First Sergeant.

'Here,' the runner answered.

      'Take this message
Back to Battalion. Are you listening?'

'Yes,' he said.

    'To Colonel Jesserman.
The Captain says we need a fifty-seven
Or tank-destroyer. Tell him that it's urgent.
Now you repeat the message.'

      Dodd did so.
He slung his rifle over his right shoulder
And climbed out of his hole.

      'Keep out of trouble,'
The sergeant said. 'Don't stop for anything.'

Dodd started to move off. The sergeant grasped
His arm: 'Watch out! They may have got patrols
Between us and Battalion. Good luck!'

Dodd waved his hand, although it was too dark
For the other to see him. And set off
In what seemed to be the right direction.

[*Rome. December 2, 1957*]

In the Suburbs

There's no way out.
You were born to waste your life.
You were born to this middleclass life

As others before you
Were born to walk in procession
To the temple, singing.

There Is

Look! From my window there's a view
of city streets
where only lives as dry as tortoises
can crawl – the Gallapagos of desire.

There is the day of Negroes with red hair
and the day of insane women on the subway;
there is the day of the word Trieste
and the night of the blind man with the electric guitar.

But I have no profession. Like a spy
I read the papers – Situations Wanted.
Surely there is a secret
which, if I knew it, would change everything!

*

I have the poor man's nerve-tic, irony.
I see through the illusions of the age!
The bell tolls, and the hearse advances,
and the mourners follow, for my entertainment.

I tread the burning pavement,
the streets where drunkards stretch
like photographs of civil death
and trumpets strangle in electric shelves.

The mannequins stare at me scornfully.
I know they are pretending
all day to be in earnest.
And can it be that love is an illusion?

When darkness falls on the enormous street
the air is filled with Eros, whispering.
Eyes, mouths, contrive to meet
in silence, fearing they may be prevented.

*

O businessmen like ruins,
bankers who are Bastilles,
widows, sadder than the shores of lakes,
then you were happy, when you still could tremble!

But all night long my window
sheds tears of light.
I seek the word. The word is not forthcoming.
O syllables of light... O dark cathedral...

A Story About Chicken Soup

In my grandmother's house there was always chicken soup
And talk of the old country – mud and boards,
Poverty,
The snow falling down the necks of lovers.

Now and then, out of her savings
She sent them a dowry. Imagine
The rice-powdered faces!
And the smell of the bride, like chicken soup.

But the Germans killed them.
I know it's in bad taste to say it,
But it's true. The Germans killed them all.

        *

In the ruins of Berchtesgaden
A child with yellow hair
Ran out of a doorway.

A German girl-child –
Cuckoo, all skin and bones –
Not even enough to make chicken soup.
She sat by the stream and smiled.

Then as we splashed in the sun
She laughed at us.
We had killed her mechanical brothers,
So we forgave her.

        *

The sun is shining.
The shadows of the lovers have disappeared.
They are all eyes; they have some demand on me –
They want me to be more serious than I want to be.

They want me to stick in their mudhole
Where no one is elegant.
They want me to wear old clothes,
They want me to be poor, to sleep in a room with many others –

Not to walk in the painted sunshine
To a summer house,
But to live in the tragic world forever.

My Father in the Night Commanding No

My father in the night commanding No
Has work to do. Smoke issues from his lips;
   He reads in silence.
The frogs are croaking and the street lamps glow.

And then my mother winds the gramophone,
The Bride of Lammermoor begins to shriek –
   Or reads a story
About a prince, a castle, and a dragon.

The moon is glittering above the hill.
I stand before the gateposts of the King –
   So runs the story –
Of Thule, at midnight when the mice are still.

And I have been in Thule! It has come true –
The journey and the danger of the world,
   All that there is
To bear and to enjoy, endure and do.

Landscapes, seascapes…where have I been led?
The names of cities – Paris, Venice, Rome –
   Held out their arms.
A feathered god, seductive, went ahead.

Here is my house. Under a red rose tree
A child is swinging; another gravely plays.
   They are not surprised
That I am here; they were expecting me.

And yet my father sits and reads in silence,
My mother sheds a tear, the moon is still,
   And the dark wind
Is murmuring that nothing ever happens.

Beyond his jurisdiction as I move
Do I not prove him wrong? And yet, it's true
   They will not change
There, on the stage of terror and of love.

The actors in that playhouse always sit
In fixed positions – father, mother, child
   With painted eyes.
How sad it is to be a little puppet!

Their heads are wooden. And you once pretended
To understand them! Shake them as you will,
   They cannot speak.
Do what you will, the comedy is ended.

Father, why did you work? Why did you weep,
Mother? Was the story so important?
   'Listen!' the wind
Said to the children, and they fell asleep.

American Poetry

Whatever it is, it must have
A stomach that can digest
Rubber, coal, uranium, moons, poems.

Like the shark it contains a shoe.
It must swim for miles through the desert
Uttering cries that are almost human.

On the Lawn at the Villa

On the lawn at the villa –
That's the way to start, eh, reader?
We know where we stand – somewhere expensive –
You and I *imperturbes*, as Walt would say,
Before the diversions of wealth, you and I *engagés*.

On the lawn at the villa
Sat a manufacturer of explosives,
His wife from Paris,
And a young man named Bruno,

And myself, being American,
Willing to talk to these malefactors,
The manufacturer of explosives, and so on,
But somehow superior. By that I mean democratic.
It's complicated, being an American,
Having the money and the bad conscience, both at the same time.
Perhaps, after all, this is not the right subject for a poem.

We were all sitting there paralysed
In the hot Tuscan afternoon,
And the bodies of the machine-gun crew were draped over the balcony.
So we sat there all afternoon.

Walt Whitman at Bear Mountain

*...life which does not give the preference to any other life, of
any previous period, which therefore prefers its own existence...*

ORTEGA Y GASSET

Neither on horseback nor seated,
But like himself, squarely on two feet,
The poet of death and lilacs
Loafs by the footpath. Even the bronze looks alive
Where it is folded like cloth. And he seems friendly.

'Where is the Mississippi panorama
And the girl who played the piano?
Where are you, Walt?
The Open Road goes to the used-car lot.

'Where is the nation you promised?
These houses built of wood sustain
Colossal snows,
And the light above the street is sick to death.

'As for the people – see how they neglect you!
Only a poet pauses to read the inscription.'

'I am here,' he answered.
'It seems you have found me out.
Yet did I not warn you that it was Myself
I advertised? Were my words not sufficiently plain?

'I gave no prescriptions,
And those who have taken my moods for prophecies
Mistake the matter.'
Then, vastly amused – 'Why do you reproach me?
I freely confess I am wholly disreputable.
Yet I am happy, because you have found me out.'

A crocodile in wrinkled metal loafing...

Then all the realtors,
Pickpockets, salesmen and the actors performing

Official scenarios,
Turned a deaf ear, for they had contracted
American dreams.

But the man who keeps a store on a lonely road,
And the housewife who knows she's dumb,
And the earth, are relieved.

All that grave weight of America
Cancelled! Like Greece and Rome.
The future in ruins!
The castles, the prisons, the cathedrals
Unbuilding, and roses
Blossoming from the stones that are not there…

The clouds are lifting from the high Sierras,
The Bay mists clearing,
And the angel in the gate, the flowering plum,
Dances like Italy, imagining red.

Lines Written Near San Francisco

I wake and feel the city trembling.
Yes, there is something unsettled in the air
And the earth is uncertain.

And so it was for the tenor Caruso.
He couldn't sleep – you know how the ovation
Rings in your ears, and you re-sing your part.

And then the ceiling trembled
And the floor moved. He ran into the street.
Never had Naples given him such a reception!

The air was darker than Vesuvius.
'*O mamma mia*,'
He cried, 'I've lost my voice!'

At that moment the hideous voice of Culture,
Hysterical woman, thrashing her arms and legs,
Shrieked from the ruins.

At that moment everyone became a performer.
Otello and Don Giovanni
And Figaro strode on the midmost stage.

In the high window of a burning castle
Lucia raved. Black horses
Plunged through fire, dragging the wild bells.

The curtains were wrapped in smoke. Tin swords
Were melting; masks and ruffs
Burned – and the costumes of the peasants' chorus.

Night fell. The white moon rose
And sank in the Pacific. The tremors
Passed under the waves. And Death rested.

2

Now, as we stand idle,
Watching the silent, bowler-hatted man,
The engineer, who writes in the smoking field;

Now as he hands the paper to a boy,
Who takes it and runs to a group of waiting men,
And they disperse and move toward their wagons,

Mules bray and the wagons move –
Wait! Before you start
(Already the wheels are rattling on the stones)

Say, did your fathers cross the dry Sierras
To build another London?
Do Americans always have to be second-rate?

Wait! For there are spirits
In the earth itself, or the air, or sea.
Where are the aboriginal American devils?

Cloud shadows, pine shadows
Falling across the bright Pacific bay...
(Already they have nailed rough boards together)

Wait only for the wind
That rustles in the eucalyptus tree.
Wait only for the light

That trembles on the petals of a rose.
(The mortar sets – banks are the first to stand)
Wait for a rose, and you may wait forever.

The silent man mops his head and drinks
Cold lemonade. 'San Francisco
Is a city second only to Paris.'

3

Every night, at the end of America
We taste our wine, looking at the Pacific.
How sad it is, the end of America!

While we were waiting for the land
They'd finished it – with gas drums
On the hilltops, cheap housing in the valleys

Where lives are mean and wretched.
But the banks thrive and the realtors
Rejoice – they have their America.

Still, there is something unsettled in the air.
Out there on the Pacific
There's no America but the Marines.

Whitman was wrong about the People,
But right about himself. The land is within.
At the end of the open road we come to ourselves.

Though mad Columbus follows the sun
Into the sea, we cannot follow.
We must remain, to serve the returning sun,

And to set tables for death.
For we are the colonists of Death –
Not, as some think, of the English.

And we are preparing thrones for him to sit,
Poems to read, and beds
In which it may please him to rest.

This is the land
The pioneers looked for, shading their eyes
Against the sun – a murmur of serious life.

The Laurel Tree

1

In the clear light that confuses everything
Only you, dark laurel,
Shadow my house,

Lifting your arms in the anguish
Of nature at the stake.
And at night, quivering with tears,

You are like the tree called Tasso's.
Crippled, and hooped with iron,
It stands on Peter's hill.

When the lovers prop their bicycles
And sit on the high benches
That look across to eternity,

That tree makes their own torsion
Seem natural. And so, they're comforted.

2

One of the local philosophers...
He says, 'In California
We have the old anarchist tradition.'

What can he mean? Is there an anarchist tradition?
And why would an anarchist want one?
O California,

Is there a tree without opinions?
Come, let me clasp you!
Let me feel the idea breathing.

I too cry O for a life of sensations
Rather than thoughts –
'The sayling Pine, the Cedar proud and tall.'

Like the girls in our neighborhood,
They're beautiful and silent.

   3

As I was digging in the back yard
I thought of a man in China.
A lifetime, it seemed, we gazed at each other.

I could see and hear his heartbeats
Like a spade hurling clods.
He pointed behind him, and I saw

That the hills were covered with armed men,
And they were all on the other side
Of the life that I held dear.

He said, 'We are as various
As the twigs of a tree,
But now the tree moves as one man.

It walks. And the earth trembles
When a race of slaves is leaving.'

   4

I said, 'Yet, all these people
Will fall down as one man
When the entrails of a bomb are breathing.

When we came down from Chosin
Carrying the guns in dainty snow-wear
And all the dead we had to,

It was a time of forgetfulness,
Like a plucked string.
It was a river of darkness.

Was it not so on your side, when you came
To the sea that was covered with ships?
Let us speak to each other,

Let the word rise, making dark strokes in the air.
That bird flies over the heads of the armed men.'

5

One part of the tree grows outward.
The other I saw when, with a light,
I explored the cellar – shattering roots.

They had broken through the wall,
As though there were something in my rubbish
That life would have at last.

I must be patient with shapes
Of automobile fenders and ketchup bottles.
These things are the beginning

Of things not visible to the naked eye.
It was so in the time of Tobit –
The dish glowed when the angel held it.

It is so that spiritual messengers
Deliver their meaning.

After Midnight

The dark streets are deserted,
With only a drugstore glowing
Softly, like a sleeping body;

With one white, naked bulb
In the back, that shines
On suicides and abortions.

Who lives in these dark houses?
I am suddenly aware
I might live here myself.

The garage man returns
And puts the change in my hand,
Counting the singles carefully.

A Son of the Romanovs

This is Avram the cello-mender,
the only Jewish sergeant
in the army of the Tsar.
One day he was mending cellos
when they shouted, 'The Tsar is coming,
everyone out or inspection!'
When the Tsar saw Avram marching
with Russians who were seven feet tall,
he said, 'He must be a genius.
I want that fellow at headquarters.'

Luck is given by God.
A wife you must find for yourself.

So Avram married a rich widow
who lived in a house in Odessa.
The place was filled with music.
Yasnaya Polyana with noodles.

One night in the middle of a concert
they heard a knock at the door.
So Avram went. It was a beggar,
a Russian, who had been blessed
by God – that is, he was crazy.
And he said, 'I'm a natural son
of the Grand Duke Nicholas.'

And Avram said, 'Eat.
I owe your people a favor.'
And he said, 'My wife is complaining
we need someone to open the door.'
So Nicholas stayed with them for years.
Who ever head of Jewish people
with a footman?

And then the Germans came. Imagine
the scene – the old people
holding onto their baggage,
and the children – they've been told it's a game,
but they don't believe it.

Then the German says, 'Who's this?'
pointing at Nicholas,
'He doesn't look like a Jew.'
And he said, 'I'm the natural son
of the Grand Duke Nicholas.'
And they saw he was feeble-minded,
and took him away too, to the death chamber.

'He could have kept his mouth shut,'
said my Grandmother,
'but what can you expect.
All of those Romanovs were a little bit crazy.'

American Dreams

In dreams my life came toward me,
my loves that were slender as gazelles.
But America also dreams....
Dream, you are flying over Russia,
dream, you are falling in Asia.

As I look down the street
on a typical sunny day in California
it is my house that is burning
and my dear ones that lie in the gutter
as the American army enters.

Every day I wake far away
from my life, in a foreign country.
These people are speaking a strange language.
It is strange to me
and strange, I think, even to themselves.

Vandergast and the Girl

Vandergast to his neighbors –
the grinding of a garage door
and hiss of gravel in the driveway.

He worked for the insurance company
whose talisman is a phoenix
rising in flames... *non omnis moriar.*
From his desk he had a view of the street –

translucent raincoats, and umbrellas,
fluorescent plate-glass windows.
A girl knelt down, arranging
underwear on a female dummy –

sea waves and, on the gale,
Venus, these busy days,
poised in her garter belt and stockings.

                    *

The next day he saw her eating
in the restaurant where he usually ate.

Soon they were having lunch together
elsewhere.

            She came from Dallas.
This was only a start, she was ambitious,
twenty-five and still unmarried.
Green eyes with silver filaments...
red hair...

            When he held the car door open
her legs were smooth and slender.

'I was wondering,'
she said, 'when you'd get round to it,'
and laughed.

                    *

Vandergast says he never intended
having an affair.

                    And was that what this was?
The names that people give to things...
What do definitions and divorce-court proceedings
have to do with the breathless reality?

O little lamp at the bedside
with views of Venice and the Bay of Naples,
you understood! *Lactona* toothbrush
and suitcase bought in a hurry,
you were the witnesses of the love
we made in bed together.

Schrafft's Chocolate Cherries, surely you remember
when she said she'd be true forever,

and, watching *Dark Storm*, we decided
there is something to be said, after all,
for soap opera, 'if it makes people happy.'

                    *

The Vandergasts are having some trouble
finding a buyer for their house.

When I go for a walk with Tippy
I pass the unweeded tennis court,
the empty garage, windows heavily shuttered.

Mrs Vandergast took the children
and went back to her family.

And Vandergast moved to New Jersey,
where he works for an insurance company
whose emblem is the Rock of Gibraltar –
the rest of his life laid out
with the child-support and alimony payments.

As for the girl, she vanished.

Was it worth it? Ask Vandergast.
You'd have to be Vandergast, looking through his eyes
at the house across the street, in Orange, New Jersey.

Maybe on wet days umbrellas and raincoats
set his heart thudding.

                       Maybe
he talks to his pillow and it whispers,
moving red hair.

In any case, he will soon be forty.

A Friend of the Family

1

Once upon a time in California
the ignorant married the inane
and they lived happily ever after.

But nowadays in the villas
with swimming pools shaped like a kidney
technicians are beating their wives.
They're accusing each other of mental cruelty.

And the children of those parents
are longing for a rustic community.
They want to get back to the good old days.

Coming toward me…a slender
sad girl dressed like a sailor…
she says, 'Do you have any change?'

One morning when the Mother Superior
was opening another can of furniture polish
Cyd ran for the bus
and came to San Francisco.
Now she drifts from pad to pad. 'Hey mister,'
she says, 'do you have any change?
I mean, for a hamburger. Really.'

2

Let Yevtushenko celebrate the construction
of a hydroelectric dam.
For Russians a dam that works is a miracle.

Why should we celebrate it?
There are lights in the mountain states,
sanatoriums, and the music of Beethoven.

Why should we celebrate the construction
of a better bowling alley?
Let Yevtushenko celebrate it.

A hundred, that's how ancient it is
with us, the rapture of material conquest,

democracy 'draining a swamp,
turning the course of a river'.

The dynamo howls
but the psyche is still, like an Indian.

And those who are still distending the empire
have vanished beyond our sight.
Far from the sense of hearing
and touch, they are merging
with Asia...

expanding the war on nature
and the old know-how to Asia.

Nowadays if we want that kind of excitement –
selling beads and whiskey to Indians,
setting up a feed store,
a market in shoes, tires, machine guns,
material ecstasy, money with hands and feet
stacked up like wooden Indians...

we must go out to Asia,
or rocketing outward in space.

3

What are they doing in Russia
these nights for entertainment?

In our desert where gas pumps shine
the women are changing their hair –
bubbles of gold and magenta...
and the young men yearning to be off
full speed...like Chichikov

in a troika-rocket, plying
the whip, while stars go flying
(Too bad for the off-beat horse!)

These nights when a space-rocket rises
and everyone sighs, 'That's Progress!'
I say to myself, 'That's Chichikov.'
As it is right here on earth –
Osteopaths on Mars,
Actuaries at the Venus-Hilton...
Chichikov talking, Chichikov eating,
Chichikov making love.

'Hey Chichikov, where are you going?'

'I'm off to the moon,' says Chichikov.

'What will you do when you get there?'

'How do I know?' says Chichikov.

4

Andrei, that fish you caught was my uncle.
He lived in Lutsk, not to be confused
with Lodz which is more famous.

When he was twenty he wrote to Chekhov,
and an answer came – 'Come to us.'
And there it was, signed 'Chekhov.'

I can see him getting on the train.
It was going to the great city
where Jews had been forbidden.

He went directly to Chekhov's house.
At the door he saw a crowd...
they told him that Chekhov had just died.

So he went back to his village.
Years passed...he danced at a wedding
and wept at a funeral.

Then, when Hitler sent for the Jews
he said, 'And don't forget Isidor...
turn left at the pickle-factory.'

Andrei, all my life I've been haunted
by Russia – a plain,
a cold wind from the *shtetl*.

I can hear the wheels of the train.
It is going to Radom,
it is going to Jerusalem.

In the night where candles shine
I have a luminous family…
people with their arms round each other
forever.

5

I can see myself getting off the train.
'Say, can you tell me how to get…'

To Chekhov's house perhaps?

That's what everyone wants, and yet
Chekhov was just a man…with ideas,
it's true. As I said to him once,
where on earth do you meet those people?

Vanya who is long-suffering
and Ivanov who is drunk.
And the man, I forget his name,
who thinks everything is forbidden…
that you have to have permission
to run, to shout…

And the people who say, 'Tell us,
what is it you do exactly to justify your existence?'

These idiots rule the world,
Chekhov knew it, and yet
I think he was happy, on his street.
People live here…you'd be amazed.

The Silent Piano

We have lived like civilised people.
O ruins, traditions!

And we have seen the barbarians,
breakers of sculpture and glass.

And now we talk of 'the inner life',
and I ask myself, where is it?

Not here, in these streets and houses,
so I think it must be found

in indolence, pure indolence,
an ocean of darkness,

in silence, an arm of the moon,
a hand that enters slowly.

*

I am reminded of a story
Camus tells, of a man in prison camp.

He had carved a piano keyboard
with a nail on a piece of wood.

And sat there playing the piano.
This music was made entirely of silence.

Venus in the Tropics

1

One morning when I went over to Bournemouth
it was crowded with American sailors –
chubby faces like Jack Oakie
chewing gum and cracking wise.

Pushing each other into the pool,
bellyflopping from the diving boards,
piling on the raft to sink it,
hanging from the rings, then letting go.

Later, when I went into Kingston
to exchange some library books,
they were everywhere, buying souvenirs,
calabash gourds, and necklaces made of seeds.

On Saturday night at the Gaiety
they kept talking and making a noise.
When the management asked them to stop
they told it to get wise, to fly a kite, to scram.

2

We drove down to Harbour Street
with Mims ('She isn't your mother.
You ought to call her by some affectionate nickname –
why don't you call her Mims?')

There were two American cruisers,
the turrets and guns distinctly visible,
and some destroyers – I counted four.

The crews were coming ashore in launches.
As each group walked off the dock
we noticed a number of women
wearing high heels. They went up to the sailors
and engaged them in conversation.

'You've seen enough,' said Mims.
'In fact, you may have seen too much.'
She started the Buick, shifting into gear
swiftly with a gloved hand.

She always wore gloves and a broad hat.
To protect her complexion, she told us.
She was extremely sensitive.
All redheaded people were.

'She's a redhead, like Clara Bow,'
our father wrote in his letter.

'The Red Death,' said my grandmother
twenty years later, on Eastern Parkway
in Brooklyn. We were talking about my father.
She thought he must have been ill –
not in his right mind – to marry a typist
and leave her practically everything.

How else to explain it, such an intelligent man?

3

The American warships left.
Then the *Empress of Britain*
came and stayed for a few days
during which the town was full of tourists.
Then, once more, the harbor was empty.

I sat by the pool at Bournemouth
reading *Typhoon*.
I had the pool all to myself,
the raft, the diving boards, and the rings.
There wasn't a living soul.

Not a voice – just rustling palm leaves
and the tops of the coconuts
moving around in circles.

In the afternoon a wind sprang up,
blowing from the sea to land,
covering the harbor with whitecaps.
It smelled of shells and seaweed,
and something else – perfume.

The Middleaged Man

There is a middleaged man, Tim Flanagan,
whom everyone calls 'Fireball'.
Every night he does the rocket-match trick.
'Ten, nine, eight...' On zero
pfft! It flies through the air.

Walking to the subway with Flanagan...
He tells me that he lives out in Queens
on Avenue Street, the end of the line.
That he 'makes his home' with his sister
who has recently lost her husband.

What is it to me?
Yet I can't help imagining what it would be like
to be Flanagan. Climbing the stairs
and letting himself in...
I can see him eating in the kitchen.

He stays up late watching television.
From time to time he comes to the window.
At this late hour the streets are deserted.
He looks up and down. He looks right at me,
then he steps back out of sight.

*

Sometimes I wake in the middle of the night
and I have a vision of Flanagan.
He is wearing an old pair of glasses
with a wire bent around the ear
and fastened to the frame with tape.

He is reading a novel by Morley Callaghan.
Whenever I wake he is still there...
with his glasses. I wish he would get them fixed.
I cannot sleep as long as there is wire
running from his eye to his ear.

Searching for the Ox

1

I have a friend who works in a mental hospital.
Sometimes he talks of his patients.
There is one, a schizophrenic:
she was born during the Korean War
and raised on an Air Force base.
Then the family moved to La Jolla.
At fourteen she started taking speed
because everyone else was taking it.

Father, I too have my cases:
hands, eyes, voices, ephemera.
They want me to see how they live.
They single me out in a crowd, at a distance,
the one face that will listen
to any incoherent, aimless story.
Then for years they hang around –
'Hey listen!' – tugging at a nerve.
Like the spirits Buddhists call
'hungry ghosts'. And when they sense an opening,
rush in. So they are born
and live. So they continue.

There is something in disorder that calls to me.
Out there beyond the harbor
where, every night, the lighthouse
probes the sea with its feathery beam,
something is rising to the surface.
It lies in the darkness breathing,
it floats on the waves regarding
this luminous world,
lights that are shining round the shoreline.
It snorts and splashes,
then rolls its blackness like a tube
back to the bottom.

At dusk when the lamps go on
I have stayed outside and watched

the shadow-life of the interior,
feeling myself apart from it.
A feeling of – as though I were made of glass.
Or the balloon I once saw in Florida
in a swimming pool, with a string
trailing in loops on the surface.
Suddenly the balloon went swiveling
on the water, trying to lift.
Then drifted steadily, being driven
from one side of the pool to the other.

2

There is a light in a window opposite.

All over the world... in China
and Africa, they are turning the pages.
All that is necessary is to submit
to engineering, law – one of the disciplines
that, when you submit, drive you forward.

There have been great strides in space.

On a flight leaving Kennedy
I have heard the engineers from IBM
speaking slide rule and doing their calculations.
I saw the first men leave for the moon:
how the rocket clawed at the ground
at first, reluctant to lift;
how it rose, and climbed, and curved,
punching a round, black hole in a cloud.

Before I got back to Orlando
it had been twice round the world.

And still, I must confess,
I fear those *messieurs*, like a peasant
listening to the priests talk Latin.
They will send me off to Heaven
when all I want is to live in the world.

3

The search for the ox continues.
I read in the *Times*, there are young men in Osaka
called Moles. They live underground
in the underground shopping center.
They cut a joint off their little finger,
and they say, 'All Al Capone.'

I have a friend who has left America –
he finds it more pleasant living in Italy.

O ruins, traditions!
Past a field full of stones,
the ruins of vine-wreathed brickwork,
the road in a soundless march continues
forever into the past.

I have sat in the field full of stones –
stones of an archway, stones
of the columns of the temple,
stones carved S.P.Q.R.,
stones that have been shaped
as women are...
Limbs of the gods that have fallen,
too cumbersome to be borne.

By the lake at Trasimeno...
If Hannibal had not paused at Trasimeno
the history of the world would have been different.
How so? There would still be a sound
of lapping water, and leaves,

4

'As you have wasted your life here in this corner
you have ruined it all over the world.'
This was written by Cavafy who lived in Alexandria.
Alexandria with blue awnings
that flap in the wind,
sea walls gleaming with reflections.
A steam winch raffles,
an anchor clanks,
smoke drifts over the rooftops,
and at night the lighted streets go sailing.

At night the gods come down –
The earth then seems so pleasant.
They pass through the murmuring crowd.
They are seen in the cafes and restaurants,
They prefer the voice of a child
or the face of a girl to their fame
in their high, cold palaces on Olympus.

In the evening the wind blows from the sea.
The wind rises and winds like a serpent
filling the diaphanous curtains
where the women sit: Mousmé,
Hélène, and the English girl.
When you pass, their lips make a sound,
twittering, like the swallows
in Cyprus that built their nests
in the temple, above the door.
Each one has a sweetheart far away.
They are making their trousseaux;
they don't make love, they knit.

In the bar down the street
a door keeps opening and closing.
Then a pair of heels go hurrying.
In the streets that lead down to the harbor
all night long there are footsteps
and opening doors. It is Eros
Peridromos, who never sleeps till dawn.

5

Following in the Way
that 'regards sensory experience as relatively unimportant',
and that aims to teach the follower
'to renounce what one is attached to' –
in spite of this dubious gift
that would end by negating poetry altogether,
in the practice of meditating
on the breath I find my awareness
of the world – the cry of a bird,
susurrus of tires, the wheezing
of the man in the chair next to me –
has increased. That every sound

falls like a pebble into a well,
sending out ripples that seem to be continuing
through the universe. Sound has a tail
that whips around the corner;
I try not to follow. In any case,
I find I am far more aware
of the present, sensory life.

I seem to understand what the artist
was driving at; every leaf stands clear
and separate. The twig seems to quiver
with intellect. Searching for the ox
I come upon a single hoofprint.
I find the ox, and tame it,
and lead it home. In the next scene
the moon has risen, a cool light.
Both the ox and herdsman vanished.

There is only earth:
in winter laden with snow,
in summer covered with leaves.

Big Dream, Little Dream

The Elgonyi say, there are big dreams and little dreams.
The little dream is just personal...
sitting in a plane that is flying
too close to the ground. There are wires...
on either side there's a wall.

The big dream feels significant.
The big dream is the kind the president has.
He wakes and tells it to the secretary,
together they tell it to the cabinet,
and before you know there is war.

Before the Poetry Reading

Composition for Voices, Dutch Banjo, Sick Flute, and a Hair Drum

1

This is the poetry reading.
This is the man who is going to give the poetry reading.
He is standing in a street in which the rain is falling
With his suitcase open on the roof of a car for some reason,
And the rain falling into the suitcase,
While the people standing nearby say,
'If you had come on a Monday,
Or a Tuesday, or a Thursday,
If you had come on a Wednesday,
Or on any day but this,
You would have had an audience,
For we here at Quinippiac (Western or Wretched State U.)
Have wonderful audiences for poetry readings.'
By this time he has closed the suitcase
And put it on the back seat, which is empty,
But on the front seat sit Saul Bellow,
James Baldwin, and Uncle Rudy and Fanya.
They are upright, not turning their heads, their fedoras straight on,
For they know where they are going,
And you should know, so they do not deign to answer
When you say, 'Where in Hell is this car going?'
Whereupon, with a leap, slamming the door shut,
Taking your suitcase with it, and your Only Available Manuscript,
And leaving you standing there,
The car leaps into the future,
Still raining, in which its taillight disappears.
And a man who is still looking on
With his coat collar turned up, says.
'If you had come on a Friday,
A Saturday or a Sunday.
Or if you had come on a Wednesday
Or a Tuesday, there would have been an audience.
For we here at Madagascar
And the University of Lost Causes
Have wonderful audiences for poetry readings.'

2

This is the man who is going to introduce you.
He says, 'Could you tell me the names
Of the books you have written.
And is there anything you would like me to say?'

3

This is the lady who is giving a party for you
After the poetry reading.
She says, 'I hope you don't mind, but
I have carefully avoided inviting
Any beautiful, attractive, farouche young women,
But the Vicar of Dunstable is coming,
Who is over here this year on an exchange program,
And the Calvinist Spiritual Chorus Society,
And all the members of the Poetry Writing Workshop.'

4

This is the man who has an announcement to make.
He says, 'I have a few announcements.
First, before the poetry reading starts,
If you leave the building and walk rapidly
Ten miles in the opposite direction,
A concert of music and poetry is being given
By Wolfgang Amadeus Mozart and William Shakespeare.
Also, during the intermission
There is time for you to catch the rising
Of the Latter Day Saints at the Day of Judgement.
Directly after the reading,
If you turn left, past the Community Building,
And walk for seventeen miles,
There is tea and little pieces of eraser
Being served in the Gymnasium.
Last week we had a reading by Dante,
And the week before by Sophocles;
A week from tonight, Saint Francis of Assisi will appear in person –
But tonight I am happy to introduce
Mister Willoughby, who will make the introduction
Of our guest, Mr...'

Working Late

A light is on in my father's study.
'Still up?' he says, and we are silent,
looking at the harbor lights,
listening to the surf
and the creak of coconut boughs.

He is working late on cases.
No impassioned speech! He argues from evidence,
actually pacing out and measuring,
while the fans revolving on the ceiling
winnow the true from the false.

Once he passed a brass curtain rod
through a head made out of plaster
and showed the jury the angle of fire –
where the murderer must have stood.
For years, all through my childhood,
if I opened a closet...bang!
There would be the dead man's head
with a black hole in the forehead.

All the arguing in the world
will not stay the moon.
She has come all the way from Russia
to gaze for a while in a mango tree
and light the wall of a veranda,
before resuming her interrupted journey
beyond the harbor and the lighthouse
at Port Royal, turning away
from land to the open sea.

Yet, nothing in nature changes, from that day to this,
she is still the mother of us all.
I can see the drifting offshore lights,
black posts where the pelicans brood.

And the light that used to shine
at night in my father's study
now shines as late in mine.

Sway

Swing and sway with Sammy Kaye.

Everyone at Lake Kearney had a nickname:
there was a Bumstead, a Tonto, a Tex,
and, from the slogan of a popular orchestra,
two sisters, Swing and Sway.

Swing jitterbugged, hopping around
on the dance floor, working up a sweat.
Sway was beautiful. My heart went out to her
when she lifted her heavy rack of dishes
and passed through the swinging door.

She was engaged, to an enlisted man
who was stationed at Fort Dix.
He came once or twice on weekends
to see her. I tried talking to him,
but he didn't answer...out of stupidity
or dislike, I could not tell which.
In real life he was a furniture salesman.
This was the hero on whom she had chosen
to bestow her affections.

I told her of my ambition:
to write novels conveying the excitement
of life...the main building lit up
like a liner on Saturday night;
the sound of the band...clarinet,
saxophone, snare drum, piano.
He who would know your heart (America)
must seek it in your songs.

And the contents of your purse...
among Kleenex, aspirin,
chewing gum wrappers, combs, et cetera.

'Don't stop,' she said, 'I'm listening.
Here it is!' flourishing her lighter.

*

In the afternoon when the dishes were washed
and tables wiped, we rowed out on the lake.
I read aloud...the *Duino Elegies*,
while she reclined, one shapely knee up,
trailing a hand in the water.

She had chestnut-colored hair.
Her eyes were changing like the surface
with ripples and the shadows of clouds.

'Beauty,' I read to her, 'is nothing
but beginning of Terror we're still just able to bear.'

*

She came from Jersey, the industrial wasteland
behind which Manhattan suddenly rises.
I could visualise the street where she lived,
and see her muffled against the cold,
in galoshes, trudging to school.
Running about in tennis shoes
all through the summer...
I could hear the porch swing squeak
and see into the parlor.
It was divided by a curtain or screen...

'That's it,' she said, 'all but the screen.
There isn't any.'

When she or her sister had a boyfriend
their mother used to stay in the parlor,
pretending to sew, and keeping an eye on them
like Fate.

At night she would lie awake
looking at the sky, spangled over.
Her thoughts were as deep and wide as the sky.
As time went by she had a feeling
of missing out...that everything
was happening somewhere else.

Some of the kids she grew up with
went crazy...like a car turning over and over.
One of her friends had been beaten
by the police. Some vital fluid
seemed to have gone out of him.
His arms and legs shook. Busted springs.

                    *

She said, 'When you're a famous novelist
will you write about me?'

I promised...and tried to keep my promise.

Recently, looking for a toolbox,
I came upon some typewritten pages,
all about her. There she is
in a canoe...a gust of wind
rustling the leaves along the shore.
Playing tennis, running up and down the baseline.
Down by the boathouse, listening to the orchestra
playing 'Sleepy Lagoon'.

Then the trouble begins. I can never think of anything
to make the characters do.
We are still sitting in the moonlight
while she finishes her cigarette.
Two people go by, talking in low voices.
A car door slams. Driving off...

'I suppose we ought to go,'
I say.
          And she says, 'Not yet.'

American Classic

It's a classic American scene –
a car stopped off the road
and a man trying to repair it.

The woman who stays in the car
in the classic American scene
stares back at the freeway traffic.

They look surprised, and ashamed
to be so helpless...
let down in the middle of the road!

To think that their car would do this!
They look like mountain people
whose son has gone against the law.

But every night they set out food
and the robber goes skulking back to the trees.
That's how it is with the car...

it's theirs, they're stuck with it.
Now they know what it's like to sit
and see the world go whizzing by.

In the fume of carbon monoxide and dust
they are not such good Americans
as they thought they were.

The feeling of being left out
through no fault of your own is common.
That's why I say, an American classic.

Why Do You Write About Russia?

When I was a child
my mother told stories about the country
she came from. Wolves were howling,
snow fell, the drunken Cossack
shouted in the snow.

Rats prowled the floor of the cellar
where the children slept.
Once, after an illness, she was sent
to Odessa, on the sea. There were battleships
painted white, and ladies and gentlemen
walking the esplanade...white naval uniforms
and parasols.

These stories were told
against a background of tropical night...
a sea breeze stirring the flowers
that open at dusk, smelling like perfume.
The voice that spoke of freezing cold
itself was warm and infinitely comforting.

So it is with poetry: whatever numbing horrors
it may speak of, the voice itself
tells of love and infinite wonder.

Later, when I came to New York,
I used to go to my grandmother's
in Brookyn. The names of stations
return in their order like a charm:
Franklin, Nostrand, Kingston.
And members of the family gather:
the three sisters, the one brother,
one of the cousins from Washington,
and myself...a 'student at Columbia.'
But what am I really?

For when my grandmother says 'Eat!
People who work with their heads have to eat more.'...
Work? Does it deserve a name
so full of seriousness and high purpose?

Gazing across Amsterdam Avenue
at the windows opposite, letting my mind
wander where it will, from the page
to Malaya, or some street in Paris...
Drifting smoke. The end will be as fatal
as an opium-eater's dream.

*

The view has changed – to evergreens
a hedge, and my neighbor's roof.
This too is like a dream, the way we live
with our cars and power mowers...
a life that shuns emotion
and the violence that goes with it,
the object being to live quietly
and bring up children to be happy.

Yes, but what are you going to tell them
of what lies ahead?
That the better life seems
the more it goes sour? The child no longer
a child, his happiness all of a sudden
behind him. And he in turn
expected to bring up his children
to be happy...

What then do I want?

A life in which there are depths
beyond happiness. As one of my friends,
Grigoryev, says, 'Two things
constantly cry out in creation,
the sea and man's soul.'

Reaching from where we are
to where we came from... *Thalassa!*
a view of the sea.

*

I sit listening to the rasp
of a power saw, the puttering of a motorboat.
The whole meaningless life around me
affirming a positive attitude...

When a hat appears, a black felt hat,
gliding along the hedge...
then a long, black overcoat
that falls beneath the knee.

He produces a big, purple handkerchief,
brushes off a chair, and sits.

'It's hot,' he says, 'but I like to walk,
that way you get to see the world.
And so, what are you reading now?'

Chekhov, I tell him.

'Of course. But have you read Leskov?
There are sentences that will stay in your mind
a whole lifetime.
For instance, in the *Lady Macbeth*,
when the woman says to her lover,
"You couldn't be nearly as desirous
as you say you are, for I heard you singing"...
he answers, "What about gnats?
They sing all their lives, but it's not for joy." '

So my imaginary friend tells stories
of the same far place the soul comes from.

When I think about Russia
it's not that area of the earth's surface
with Leningrad to the West and Siberia
to the East – I don't know anything
about the continental mass.

It's a sound, such as you hear
in a sea breaking along a shore.

My people came from Russia,
bringing with them nothing
but that sound.

Typhus

'The whole earth was covered with snow,
and the Snow Queen's sleigh came gliding.
I heard the bells behind me,
and ran, and ran, till I was out of breath.'

During the typhus epidemic
she almost died, and would have
but for the woman who lived next door
who cooked for her and watched by the bed.

When she came back to life
and saw herself in a mirror
they had cut off all her hair.
Also, they had burned her clothing,
and her doll, the only one she ever had,
made out of rags and a stick.

Afterwards, they sent her away
to Odessa, to stay with relatives.
The day she was leaving for home
she bought some plums, as a gift
to take back to the family.
They had never seen such plums!
They were in a window, in a basket.
To buy them she spent her last few kopecks.

The journey took three days by train.
It was hot, and the plums were beginning to spoil.
So she ate them...
until, finally, all were gone.
The people on the train were astonished.
A child who would eat a plum
and cry... then eat another!

                    *

Her sister, Lisa, died of typhus.
The corpse was laid on the floor.

They carried it to the cemetery
in a box, and brought back the box.
'We were poor – a box was worth something.'

89

The Art of Storytelling

Once upon a time there was a shocket,
that is, a kosher butcher,
who went for a walk.

He was standing by the harbor
admiring the ships, all painted white,
when up came three sailors, led by an officer.
'Filth,' they said, 'who gave you permission?'
and they seized and carried him off.

So he was taken into the navy.
It wasn't a bad life – nothing is.
He learned how to climb and sew,
and to shout 'Glad to be of service, Your Excellency!'
He sailed all round the world,
was twice shipwrecked, and had other adventures.
Finally, he made his way back to the village…
whereupon he put on his apron, and picked up his knife,
and continued to be a shocket.

At this point, the person telling the story
would say, 'This shocket-sailor
was one of our relatives, a distant cousin.'

It was always so, they knew they could depend on it.
Even if the story made no sense,
the one in the story would be a relative –
a definite connection with the family.

Caviare at the Funeral

This was the village where the deacon ate all the caviare at the funeral.
CHEKHOV, 'In the Ravine'

On the way back from the cemetery
they discussed the funeral arrangements
and the sermon, 'such a comfort to the family'.

They crowded into the parlor.
It was hot, and voices were beginning to rise.
The deacon found himself beside a plate
heaped with caviare. He helped himself
to a spoonful. Then another.

Suddenly he became aware
that everyone's eyes were upon him,
ruin staring him in the face.
He turned pale. Then tried to carry it off –
one may as well be hanged for a sheep
as a lamb, et cetera.

Meeting their eyes with a stern expression
he took another spoonful, and another.
He finished the plate.

Next morning he was seen at the station
buying a ticket for Kurovskoye,
a village much like ours, only smaller.

Chocolates

Once some people were visiting Chekhov.
While they made remarks about his genius
the Master fidgeted. Finally
he said, 'Do you like chocolates?'

They were astonished, and silent.
He repeated the question,
whereupon one lady plucked up her courage
and murmured shyly, 'Yes.'

'Tell me,' he said, leaning forward,
light glinting from his spectacles,
'what kind? The light, sweet chocolate
or the dark, bitter kind?'

The conversation became general
They spoke of cherry centers,
of almonds and Brazil nuts.
Losing their inhibitions
they interrupted one another.
For people may not know what they think
about politics in the Balkans,
or the vexed question of men and women,

but everyone has a definite opinion
about the flavor of shredded coconut.
Finally someone spoke of chocolates filled with liqueur,
and everyone, even the author of *Uncle Vanya*,
was at a loss for words.

As they were leaving he stood by the door
and took their hands.
                    In the coach returning to Petersburg
they agreed that it had been a most
unusual conversation.

Armidale

Il faut voyager loin en aimant sa maison.
APOLLINAIRE

1 *As a Man Walks*

It's a strange country,
strange for me to have come to.
Cattle standing in a field,
sheep that are motionless
as stones,
the sun sinking in a pile of clouds,
and the eternal flies
getting in your ears and eyes...

I suppose you become accustomed.
Mrs Scully was in her kitchen
entertaining two friends
when one said, 'Isn't that a snake?'
and pointed. Sure enough
one was sliding around the divider.
She reached for something, the rolling pin,
and stunned it. Then finished it off
with a hammer.

The green-hide and stringy-bark Australian...
my candidate for survival
in the event of fire, flood,
or nuclear explosion.

As a man walks he creates the road he walks on.
All of my life in America
I must have been reeling out of myself
this red dirt, gravel road.

Three boys seated on motorcycles
conferring...

A little further on,
a beaten-up Holden parked off the road
with two men inside passing the bottle.
Dark-skinned…maybe aboriginal.
I might have been content to live
in Belle Terre, among houses and lawns,
but inside me are gum trees,
and magpies, cackling and whistling,
and a bush-roaming kangaroo.

2 *A Bush Band*

A guitar and drum,
a pole with bottlecaps nailed to it…

Struck with a piece of wood
it gives off a silvery, joyful sound.

The woman playing the guitar
is sinewy, like the men in the ballad.

Driving their cattle overland
from Broome to Glen Garrick…

Cows low, wagon wheels turn,
red dust hangs in the air.

Some give their lives to cattle
and some to the words of a song,

arriving together at Glen Garrick
and at the end of the song.

Back in the States

It was cold, and all they gave him to wear
was a shirt. And he had malaria.

There was continual singing of hymns –
'Nearer My God to Thee' was a favorite.
And a sound like running water...
it took him a while to figure it.

Weeping, coming from the cells
of the men who had been condemned.

Now here he was, back in the States,
idly picking up a magazine,
glancing through the table of contents.

Already becoming like the rest of us.

FROM **THE BEST HOUR OF THE NIGHT** (1983)

How to Live on Long Island

Lilco, $75.17;
Mastercard, $157.89;
Sunmark Industries, $94.03…
Jim is paying his bills.
He writes out a check
and edges it into the envelope
provided by the company.
They always make them too small.

The print in the little box
in the top right corner informs him:
'The Post Office will not deliver
mail without proper postage.'
They seem to know that the public
is composed of thieves and half-wits.

He seals the last envelope,
licks a stamp, sticks it on,
and with a feeling of virtue,
a necessary task accomplished,
takes the checks out to the mailbox.

It's a cool, clear night in Fall,
lights flickering through the leaves.
He thinks, All these families
with their situation comedies:
husbands writing checks,
wives studying fund-raising,
children locked in their rooms
listening to the music that appeals to them,
remind me of… fireflies
that shine for a night and die.

Of all these similar houses
what shall be left? Not even stones.
One could almost understand the pharaohs
with their pyramids and obelisks.

Every month when he pays his bills
Jim Bandy becomes a philosopher.
The rest of the time he's OK.

Jim has a hobby: fishing.
Last year he flew to Alaska.
Cold the salmon stream,
dark the Douglas firs,
and the pure stars are cold.

A bear came out of the forest.
Jim had two salmon... he threw one
but the bear kept coming.
He threw the other... it stopped.

The fish that are most memorable
he mounts, with a brass plate
giving the name and place and date:
Chinook Salmon, Red Salmon,
Brown Trout, Grouper,
Barracuda, Hammerhead Shark.
They do a lot of drinking in Alaska.
He saw thirty or forty lying drunk
in the street. And on the plane...

They cannot stand living in Alaska,
and he cannot stand Long Island
without flying to Alaska.

Quiet Desperation

At the post office he sees Joe McInnes.
Joe says. 'We're having some people over.
It'll be informal. Come as you are.'

She is in the middle
of preparing dinner. Tonight
she is trying an experiment:
Hal Burgonyaual – Fish-Potato Casserole.
She has cooked and drained the potatoes
and cut the fish in pieces.
Now she has to 'mash potatoes,
add butter and hot milk', et cetera.

He relays Joe's invitation.
'No,' she says, 'not on your life.
Muriel McInnes is no friend of mine.'

It appears that she told Muriel
that the Goldins live above their means,
and Muriel told Mary Goldin.

He listens carefully, to get things right.
The feud between the Andersons and the Kellys
began with Ruth Anderson calling Mike Kelly
a reckless driver. Finally
the Andersons had to sell their house and move.

Social life is no joke.
It can be the only life there is.

*

In the living room the battle of Iwo Jima
is in progress, watched by his son.
Men are dying on the beach,
pinned down by a machine gun.

The marine carrying the satchel charge
falls. Then Sergeant Stryker
picks up the charge and starts running.

Now you are with the enemy machine gun
firing out of the pillbox
as Stryker comes running,
bullets at his heels kicking up dust.
He makes it to the base of the pillbox,
lights the charge, raises up,
and heaves it through the opening.
The pillbox explodes...
the NCOs wave, 'Move out!'
And he rises to his feet.
He's seen the movie. Stryker gets killed
just as they're raising the flag.

                              *

A feeling of pressure...
There is something that needs to be done
immediately.

                  But there is nothing,
only himself. His life is passing,
and afterwards there will be eternity,
silence, and infinite space.

He thinks, Firewood! –
and goes to the basement,
takes the Swede saw off the wall,
and goes outside, to the woodpile.

He carries an armful to the sawhorse
and saws the logs into smaller pieces.
In twenty minutes he has a pile of firewood
cut just the right length.
He carries the cut logs into the house
and arranges them in a neat pile
next to the fireplace.

Then looks around for something else to do,
to relieve the feeling of pressure.

The dog!
He will take the dog for a walk.

                              *

They make a futile procession...
he commanding her to 'Heel!' –
she dragging back or straining ahead.

The leaves are turning yellow.
Between the trunks of the trees
the cove is blue, with ripples.
The swans – this year there are seven –
are sailing line astern.

But when you come closer
the rocks above the shore are littered
with daggers of broken glass
where the boys sat on summer nights
and broke beer bottles afterwards.

And the beach is littered,
with cans, containers, heaps of garbage,
newspaper wadded against the sea-wall.
Someone has even dumped a mattress...
a definite success!

Some daring guy, some Stryker
in the pickup speeding away.

He cannot bear the sun
going over and going down...
the trees and houses vanishing
in quiet every day.

The Previous Tenant

1

All that winter it snowed.
The sides of roads were heaped with it.
The nights were quiet. If you stepped outside,
above the dark woods and fields
hung glittering stars and constellations.

My landlord, Stanley, came by now and then
to see how things were going.
I reminded him that the previous tenant
had left boxes full of clothes,
a pair of skis, a rifle,
three shelves of books, and a fishing pole.

All right, he said, he'd get in touch with him.
I said, he must have left in a hurry.

A hurry? Stanley considered.
His eyes gleamed under bushy eyebrows.
Satanic. But I happened to know that Stanley
wouldn't hurt a fly. All that Fall
I'd seen him trying to think of something
to persuade some raccoons to quit the premises –
everything short of a gun.

'McNeil was a bit disorganised,'
he said with a smile.
I asked if he'd like some coffee,
and he said yes. While I was making it
he talked about the previous tenant.

2

A doctor named Hugh McNeil
came on the staff at Mercy Hospital
and bought a house in Point Mercy.

Hugh and Nancy fitted right in...
people liked them.
Helen Knox, whose husband was vice-president

of the National Maritime Bank,
called on Nancy and invited her
to join the Garden Club.
Then they were asked to join the Golf Club.
(The Levines, on the other hand, hadn't been invited.
After two years of Point Mercy
they sold their house and moved back to Queens.)

The McNeils had children: Tom, fourteen,
and Laurie, nine and a half, nearly ten.
McNeil was one of the fathers on Saturday
dashing about. He drove a green Land Rover
as though he were always on safari
with the children and an Irish setter.

Nancy was nice…blonde,
and intelligent – she'd been to Wellesley.
She took on the job of secretary
of the Garden Club, that nobody wanted,
and helped organise the dance at the Yacht Club
on July the Fourth, for Hugh had joined that too.
He bought a 'Cal' Thirty Martini-rigged sloop,
and with Tom as crew went sailing.
They came in fifth in the Martha Woodbury
Perpetual Trophy.

       Nancy didn't sail,
it made her seasick. She sat on the patio
with her knitting till the boats hove in sight,
then went down to the basin.

McNeil spoke at village meetings
with moderation and common sense.
Once he argued for retaining
the Latin teacher at the high school.
Latin, he explained, was still useful
for medicine and law, and a foundation
for good English. They heard him out
and voted to let the Latin teacher go
and remodel the gymnasium.
McNeil accepted defeat gracefully.
That was one of the things they liked about him.

The residents of Point Mercy
are proud of their village
with its beautiful homes and gardens
and wild life sanctuary.
Contrary to what people say
about the suburbs, they appreciate culture.
Hugh McNeil was an example…
doing the shopping, going to the club,
a man in no way different from themselves,
husband and family man
and good neighbor, who nevertheless spoke Latin.

   3

Her name was Irene Davis.
Before she married it was Cristiano.
'I met her once,' said Helen Knox.
'Harry introduced her to me
at the bank. A dark woman…
I think, a touch of the tar brush.'

There is no accounting for tastes
observed Sandie Bishop.

The woman's husband was an invalid
and patient of Dr McNeil.
The green Land Rover had been seen
parked outside the Davis house
in the afternoon, in the evening, and once –
this was hilarious – the doctor
ran out of gas in that part of town
at three in the morning. He didn't have cash
or credit cards on him, and had to walk
to the nearest open service station.
The attendant let him have a gallon.
'I've been in the same fix,' he told McNeil,
'you can pay me some other time.'

The attendant talked, and the story
got back to Point Mercy.
'It's a scandal,' said Sandie.
'Do you think Nancy knows?'
Helen said, 'I'm sure she does.'

'Someone should have a talk with him,'
Sandie said. She remembered
with some excitement, the occasion
when a resident of Point Mercy
had been thinking of selling his house
to a family that was black.
Every morning he would find garbage
dumped on his lawn. The prospective buyer
received an anonymous letter,
and that was the end of that.
'Let's not be hasty,' said Helen
who was president of the Garden Club
and had more experience.
'These things have a way of working themselves out.'

    4

One day there was a sensation:
Dr McNeil had been mugged,
beaten and left by the road.

'Mugged?' said the service station attendant.
This was long after the event.

He looked around, but there was no one
in hearing distance, only the dog,
a hound that wandered around
with an infected ear, snapping at flies.
All at once it perked up its ears
and went running. It must have smelled something
mixed with the odor of gasoline
and dust... a delirious
fragrance of sensual life.

The attendant leaned closer
and said in a conspiratorial voice,
'He was never mugged.
It was Irene Davis's brothers,
the Cristianos. They had him beat up.'

He knew about gangsters. They would beat up a guy
to warn him. The next time it was curtains.

5

So McNeil was in the hospital
with two broken ribs, black eyes,
and a missing tooth.

At the next meeting of the Garden Club
the president said she was as broad-minded
as anyone, but this...
here she paused as though it were beneath her
to find words for such low behavior...
had brought violence into their midst.

Sandie moved they send a delegation
to the hospital, to demand
McNeil's immediate resignation.

The next day four of the members
called on Dr Abrahams, chief of staff,
and told him what they wanted.
A short man, with hair on his face,
all the time they were talking he kept turning
from one to the other, and grinning
like some sort of monkey,
Sandie said afterwards.

He thanked them for their concern.
But McNeil's private life –
not that he knew anything about it –
had nothing to do with his work
or his position here at the hospital.
If they would take his advice
they would be careful what they said –
they might find themselves charged
with libel. Speaking, he was sure,
for the entire staff, they were fortunate
to have a surgeon of Hugh McNeil's caliber.

Could he be of service in anything else?
No? Then would they please excuse him...
it looked like a busy day.

They were halfway to the parking lot.

'What can you expect?' said Helen.
'It was bad enough letting them in,
but to make one chief of staff!'

She knew how to put what they were feeling
into words. This was why
she was president – elected not once
or twice…this was her third term in office.

6

Then Nancy sued for divorce.
She had all the evidence she needed:
her husband had been with Irene Davis
in Providence, Rhode Island,
when he was supposed to be in Boston
attending a medical conference.

This was when he moved into the cottage.
It consisted of a small bedroom,
living room, bathroom, kitchen.
Thoreau, who recommends sleeping in the box
railroad workers keep their tools in,
would have found this house commodious.

I could imagine him coming home…
putting some fries on a metal sheet
and sliding it into the oven
set at 350 degrees.
Sprinkling a couple of chops
with pepper and garlic.
Deciding which frozen vegetable…
say, spinach. Putting the block
in a saucer with water and salt.
Making a salad…but this would mean
slicing tomatoes, radishes, scallions,
and washing lettuce. There would be times
when he just couldn't be bothered.

He would have a drink, then a second.
You have to be careful not to make it three
and four. On the other hand
you shouldn't be too careful,

or like Robinson Crusoe you may find yourself
taking pride in the neatness and efficiency
of your domestic arrangements:
all your bowls made out of gourds
lined up on a shelf according to size.
Ditto your spoons.
'A place for everything,' you say to the parrot,
'and everything in its place.'

Bake the French fries,
boil the frozen vegetable, broil the lamb chops.
You can prepare a nourishing dinner
in twenty minutes, and eat it in five
while reading the *Times* or watching *Charlie's Angels*.
He would watch TV again after dinner.
My God, he'd say to the walls,
it can't be this bad. But it was.
He'd turn it off and pick up a book.
Now that he had plenty of time
he could catch up on the ones he'd missed
when they came out: titles like *Future Shock*
and *The Greening of America*.

Then he was on an express train
racing to the end of the line,
a flash and a moment of excruciating
pain. He was paralysed,
helpless to move a leg or an arm.

And woke, having fallen asleep
in his chair, to hear the dripping
of snow melting on the roof.

On nights when he couldn't sleep
he'd watch the late late show.
In the dark night of the soul,
says F. Scott Fitzgerald,
it is always three in the morning.
Hemingway says, it isn't so bad...
in fact, the best hour of the night
once you've reconciled yourself to insomnia
and stopped worrying about your sins.

And I say that insomnia can be
a positive joy if you're tuned into *Dames*
or *Gold Diggers of 1933*.
I remember seeing *The Producers*
at three in the morning and practically
falling out of bed. There are pleasures
known to none but late late movie-goers,
moments of the purest absurdity,
such as, in an otherwise boring movie
starring the Marx Brothers, the 'Tenement Symphony'
as sung by Tony Martin.

So there he was, watching Busby Berkeley's
electrically lighted waterfalls,
and the Warner Brothers cuties
viewed from underneath, treading water.

'Ain't we got fun!' shrieked the parrot,
and the goat gave a great bound.

7

Behind the Perry Masons and Agatha Christies
I came across a packet of letters.
It was like being a detective.

When Irene's husband came home
from the hospital, he was confined
to his bed, by doctor's orders.
And McNeil was the doctor.
'Call me at home,' said Irene.
'There is no problem about telephone calls.'

I copied some of the passages –
they might come in useful.
There was an idea for a novel
I'd had for years: *A Bovary of the Sierras*...
The Bovary of Evanston... *The Bovary of Green Harbor*.

There was a paragraph about some flowers
and his cock that might have been conceived
by the author of *Lady Chatterley's Lover*.
It went to show that when an idea

has genuine merit, individuals
far removed in space and time
come upon it independently.

She even knew her Bible:
'When my beloved slipped his hand through the latch-hole
my bowels stirred within me.'

Rumor was right. It was her brothers
who had McNeil beaten up.
She told him that he wasn't to see her
ever again. She feared for his life.
'Irene...signing off.'

But she didn't sign off. Here she was again.
'If you have a new woman in your life
or you've gone back to your wife
I don't want to muck things up.
This is just a peacepipe, kid –
send me a smoke signal
if I'm getting in the way of anything.
Cheerio, Irene.'

Then they picked up again where they'd left off.
They had been with each other yesterday.
She could still feel him inside her.

I was beginning to be afraid
for him. For her. For both of them.

8

Stanley telephoned to say that McNeil
was coming to pick up his things.

I put the books in cartons,
and piled the cartons and the rest of his things
next to the door: the boxes of clothes,
the skis, the fishing pole,
and the rifle – I was loath to part with it,
the way America was greening.

The next day my predecessor
arrived. A man of forty
with red hair... looking slightly angry.
Suspicious. I couldn't put my finger on it.

He was accompanied by a young woman
wearing jeans and a sweater.
She was fair, and had a friendly smile.
'It was good of you to take care
of Hugh's things,' she said. 'Wasn't it, Hugh?'
'O yes,' he said. 'Thanks.'

I helped them carry things out
to the station wagon. It was snowing again...
not flakes but particles, coming down fast
at an angle, like rain or hail.

They drove away.
She waved. He looked straight ahead.
It appeared he was back on the track
once more, after his derailment.
With a woman of the right kind at his side
to give him a nudge. 'Say thanks!'

9

It is always that famous day and year
at the Colony Inn... a brick fireplace,
rough-hewn beams, and pewter candlesticks.
From the ceiling hang the flags
of the thirteen original colonies.

The waitresses wear bonnets and muslin gowns
that hang straight from the shoulder
to the floor, leaving their arms and elbows
exposed. Some of the older waitresses
seem to resent being made to dress
like children. Their movements are slow.

One of them arrived finally
to take our order and departed,
moving with slow steps
as befitted an early American.

Maggie said, 'Don't look now!
By the window...that's Irene Davis,
the woman McNeil had the affair with.'

I looked around the room casually
and let my gaze come to rest
on Irene.

They said she was dark. What they hadn't said
was that the darkness, jet black hair,
was set off by a skin like snow,
like moonlight in a dark field.
Her features were...fine. She wouldn't have been
out of place in an Italian villa
with walls five feet thick, and chickens
roosting on the furniture...the family
crowded into three rooms upstairs...
a contessa, married to the invalid son
of impoverished aristocracy.

I wondered what she would have thought
if she'd known I'd read her letters.

There were two people with her:
an old woman with white hair
who looked as though she'd just got off
the boat from Palermo...
and a man, he must be Irene's brother...
the same black hair and white complexion.
But what in her looked romantic,
in him spelled murder. He was thin
and sinewy...wearing a green jacket,
dark green shirt, white tie.

I imagined he was being tolerant
of the restaurant...these assholes
with their consommés and casseroles,
their salads consisting of lettuce and
cottage cheese. And what was this
for chrissake? Sweet potato
with marshmallow on top...you call this food?

But he was on his best behavior.
He didn't pull an automatic
and blow holes through the flags
of the thirteen original colonies.

Irene must have felt me staring.
She turned...her eyes met mine
for a few seconds. I had an impression
of...defiance. 'What do you want?'

I quickly looked away.

10

Maggie was meeting a friend
at three. It was now two-thirty.
So we walked around Island Bay.

The village has been reconstructed
to preserve a Colonial atmosphere.
At the crest of a slope facing the bay
stands the post office. This at least
is authentic. It has four columns,
white of course, and a big golden eagle
above the entrance. On either side
in a crescent there are shops
with signs lettered in gold:
Optometrist, Pharmacy, Antiques...
There's a shop selling Irish linen
and wool. Another selling jewelry
and notions...Royal Doulton...
little statues of Colonial women
in hoopskirts and wigs,
and the figure of a young girl
in shorts, taking a swing at a golf ball.

The slope goes down to a road.
Between this and the bay
stands a gazebo, an open dome
housing a bust of Hercules.
This, they say, was a ship's figurehead.
All but the bearded head
is a reconstruction...some local artist

has added a muscular torso
and draped over one shoulder
the skin of the Nemean lion.
A sillier, more pathetic monster
it would be hard to imagine,
with his doggy nose and wide-open eyes
that seem to say, Look at me.
I never did any harm.

This monument to our culture,
believe it or not, had been vandalised…
battered and gashed.
Whoever did it must have used a hammer
or an axe.

I said, 'Boys will be boys.'

'I'm sure,' Maggie said, 'it wasn't anyone
from around here.'

I wasn't so sure. Our high schools
every year turn out their quota of vandals
and thieves. Not to mention illiterates.
You don't have to go into New York City…

How, she said, could I be so cynical?

I said, why was it that when you told the truth
people accused you of being cynical?

We were on our way to having a quarrel.
I didn't want to. I liked Maggie,
with her quizzical way of looking at me,
her air of calm, unclouded judgment,
her mouth that turned down at one corner
when she smiled.

But now she wasn't smiling.
She said, 'It's your attitude.
Like what you said in the restaurant
about Hugh McNeil and the Davis woman
being better than the rest of us.'

She had her back to the post office.
The wings of the golden eagle
seemed to spring out of her shoulders.

I was filled with a sense of the ridiculous.
She sensed it, and became really angry.
'I know, you prefer vulgar people.
Anyone who tries to be decent and respectable
is either a hypocrite or a fool.'

So we had our quarrel.
Then a car drove up and stopped.
It was Helen Knox. She leaned over
and opened the door for Maggie.

'Good afternoon,' she said to me,
very cool. I knew what she thought of me
and my writing. A friend told me –
for writers have such friends.

She said, 'I thought I ought to read
one of his novels. But I couldn't bring myself
to finish it. Why write about
such ordinary things?

What with chauffeuring the children
and entertaining Harry's friends,
if I find time to read, it has to be something
that takes me out of myself.

You have to be selective –
this is why I read *The New Yorker*, and *Time*
and subscribe to the Book of the Month.'

The Eleventh Commandment

'Do you know the eleventh commandment?'
Harry asks. I shake my head.
I'm the straight man in these encounters.

'The eleventh commandment,'
he says, 'is, "Don't get caught".'

Then, as I recall, everyone laughs.

*

He hands a hundred-dollar bill
to his older boy, to buy fireworks
from a man from New Jersey
who's selling them out of his truck.

Then he and I and the boys
are setting them off. Rockets
go climbing with a whoosh
and bang! The sky above Green Harbor
is lit red, white, and blue.
Bright flares come glimmering down.
People have come out of their houses
and stand in the street, looking up.

A thoroughly illegal operation
that everyone is taking part in...
What could be more appropriate
on the Fourth of July? More American?

*

If you want to accomplish anything
in this world, you can't be too particular.
Ethics are nice to have on a wall, in Latin,
but Latin won't meet a payroll.
And don't give me any of that
about the system. It's the same in Russia.

*

When the financial scandal burst
in the light of the flash he was still smiling,
'confident that he and his partners
would be cleared of all violations' –

kickbacks, misapplication of funds,
conspiracy, fraud, concealment, wire fraud,
falsified books and records, and
interstate transportation of stolen property.

*

'I miss him,' she says.

'What makes me sick
is the way everyone's turned against him.

Let me tell you about the people
next door. They're stealing bricks
from a building site. Every night
they drive over and steal some more.
They're making a patio and an outdoor barbecue.'

Her younger boy, Kyle, comes over
and stands watchfully in front of me.
He is wearing a spaceman's helmet
and carrying a ray gun or laser.

'Hi there,' I say to him.
What else do you say to a six-year-old?

Ed

Ed was in love with a cocktail waitress,
but Ed's family, and his friends,
didn't approve. So he broke it off.

He married a respectable woman
who played the piano. She played well enough
to have been a professional.

Ed's wife left him...
Years later, at a family gathering
Ed got drunk and made a fool of himself.

He said, 'I should have married Doreen.'
'Well,' they said, 'why didn't you?'

Akhmatova's Husband

Akhmatova's husband, Gumilev,
was a poet and an explorer.
He wrote poems about wild animals
and had fantastic ideas:
a red bird with the head of a girl
and a lost tram that goes wandering,

shedding fire 'like a storm with dark wings',
passing over bridges,
by a house with three windows
where a woman he loved once lived,
and, rushing toward him,
two raised hooves and an iron glove.

Gumilev fought in the Great War
with almost incredible valor,
twice winning the Cross of Saint George.
He envisioned a little old man
forging the bullet that would kill him.

It wasn't a German bullet, it was Russian.
Gumilev was killed by his own countrymen
as poets in Russia frequently are.

Everyone talks about Akhmatova
but no one talks about Gumilev.
That wouldn't have mattered to Gumilev.
When the man from the government came to kill him,
'Just give me a cigarette,' said Gumilev,
'and let's get it over with.'

The Unwritten Poem

You will never write the poem about Italy.
What Socrates said about love
is true of poetry – where is it?
Not in beautiful faces and distant scenery
but the one who writes and loves.

In your life here, on this street
where the houses from the outside
are all alike, and so are the people.
Inside, the furniture is dreadful –
flock on the walls, and huge color television.

To love and write unrequited
is the poet's fate. Here you'll need
all your ardor and ingenuity.
This is the front and these are the heroes –
a life beginning with 'Hi!' and ending with 'So long!'

You must rise to the sound of the alarm
and march to catch the 6:20 –
watch as they ascend the station platform
and, grasping briefcases, pass beyond your gaze
and hurl themselves into the flames.

The People Next Door

He isn't a religious man.
So instead of going to church
on Sunday they go to sea.

They cruise up and down,
see the ferry coming from Bridgeport
to Green Harbor, and going back
from Green Harbor to Bridgeport...
and all the boats there are.
The occasional silent fisherman...
When the kids start to get restless
he heads back to shore.

I hear them returning
worn out and glad to be home.
This is as close to being happy
as a family ever gets.
I envy their content. And yet
I've done that too, and know
that no hobby or activity
distracts one from thinking
forever. Every human being
is an intellectual more or less.

I too was a family man.
It was a phase I had to go through.
I remember tenting in the Sierras,
getting up at dawn to fly cast.
I remember my young son
almost being blown off the jetty
in Lochalsh. Only the suitcase
he was carrying held him down.
The same, at Viareggio,
followed me into the sea
and was almost swept away by the current.

These are the scenes I recall
rather than Christmas and Thanksgiving.
My life as the father of a family
seems to have been a series
of escapes, not to mention illnesses,
confrontations with teachers,
administrators, police.
Flaubert said, 'They're in the right,'
looking at a bourgeois family,
and then went back happily
to his dressing gown and pipe.

Yes, I believe in the family...
next door. I rejoice
at their incomings and outgoings.
I am present when Betty
goes out on her first date.
I hear about Joey's being chosen
for the team. I survive the takeover
of the business, and the bad scare
at the doctor's.
I laugh with them that laugh
and mourn with them that mourn.

I see their lights, and hear a murmur
of voices from house to house.

It gives me a strange feeling
to think how far they've come
from some far world to this,
bending their necks to the yoke
of affection.

                And that one day,
with a few simple words
and flowers to keep them company
they'll return once more to the silence
out there, beyond the stars.

White Oxen

A man walks beside them
with a whip that he cracks.
The cart they draw is painted
with Saracens and Crusaders,
fierce eyes and ranks of spears.

They are on the steep road
that goes up the mountain.
Their neat-stepping hoofs
appear to be flickering
in the sun, raising dust.

They are higher than the roofs
on which striped gourds and melons
lie ripening. They move
among the dark green olives
that grow on the rocks.

They dwindle as they climb...
vanish around a corner
and reappear walking on the edge
of a precipice. They enter
the region of mist and darkness.

I think I can see them still:
a pair of yoked oxen
the color of ivory
or smoke, with red tassels,
in the gathering dusk.

A Bramble Bush

One night in winter Willa went missing.
I took my Irish raincoat, gloves,
and a flashlight.

            In half an hour
I had her and the wood had me,
caught in brambles. I couldn't use my hands –
if I set her down she'd run off again.
So I stood there, seeing the irony,
lights only a hundred yards away,
and hearing sounds of television:
the murmur of a voice, or voices,
followed by a roar of applause…
some situation comedy or stand-up comedian.

                    *

Winter has passed, and it is spring again
when the small green buds with forked tails
like fishes swim on the wind.
Then summer, gold on green…
Looking at the sky through the leaves
is like looking through shining crystal.

Then the leaves come drifting down,
and it's December. Frau Holle
fills the sky with white feathers.
Rain falls and freezes. The boughs are sheathed
in ice, with bright icicles hanging down
like lace. The whole wood glitters.

                    *

After some prolonged litigation
between the Town and the man who owns the land
the wood stands on, it has been agreed
to cut the trees down and build houses.
The development is to be called Birchwood
and zoned for half or quarter acres.

And so, one spring, comes the surveyor
squinting through his telescope. 'Joe,'
he shouts, 'look behind you!
What's that in the bush?'

Joe looks and sees,
tangled in thorns, the skeleton of a man
still holding the skeleton of a dog.

*

A cold gust of air set the wood rustling.
Lightning flashed. There was a roll of thunder.
But this was not my kind of story.
I turned around with my back to the brambles
and, holding the dog to my chest,
hurled myself backward.

They gave a little. I did it again...
and so, standing and falling, made lunatic progress
until I fell out of a bush into the open.

I rested a while, then put her on the leash,
and walked the short way home, arriving
as the first cold raindrops fell.

Sea of Grass

(for Jimmy Ernst)

If you're a Jew and want to know
which transport your mother was on,
the French railroads have a list.
Jimmy showed me the name of his:
'Lou Straus-Ernst...Transport 76.'

One of those who made the journey
and survived, gave an account:
'Seventy would be put in a boxcar.
There would be a long wait
while the train was boarded up.
Then three days' travel east...
paper mattresses on the floor
for the sick, bare boards for the rest.
Many did not survive.'

*

At Auschwitz shortly before the end
one had seen her: 'A woman totally exhausted,
half lying, half leaning against a wall,
warming herself in the last rays of a dying sun.'

And still we believe in loving-kindness...
some even believe there's a God.
This is a mystery, *ein Rätsel*
God himself could not explain.

*

A few minutes' walk from the house
where I live, there's a beach,
a brown strip of sand
lined with tide-wrack and litter...
boards, plastic bottles
and, at the water's edge, green reeds.

'Sea of Grass' Jimmy called it.
Every time I come here I think of him
and his painting.

       'Work!
God wants you to,' said Flaubert.

There they are every summer
just as he painted them,
growing up again...a hedge
of stems and leaves standing motionless.

Blue water, and a harbor's mouth
opening into the sky.

FROM **THERE YOU ARE** (1995)

Suddenly

Nipkow and Cosulich
exported "seconds", merchandise
with small imperfections...
nylon stockings, ballpoint pens.
I packed them in cellophane,
then cartons, to be shipped
to Europe for their postwar legs
and literary movements.

Nipkow had a sideline, diamonds.
He would sit at his desk by the hour
holding a diamond up to the light
or staring at some little diamonds
in the palm of his left hand.
He'd rise and grind a diamond
on the wheel. Then put on his coat
and go to meet someone like himself
with whom he would exchange diamonds,
each of them making a profit
somehow out of this.

One day I suddenly quit.
Then I worked on the *Herald Tribune*.
A reporter would call 'Copyboy!'
and one of us would run over
and take his copy to the horseshoe
where the Count, as we named him,
a bald head and rimless glasses,
presided over his crew.

One would read the piece in a hurry
and write a heading for it,
so many letters to fit.

My greatest adventure
was going to the fourteenth floor
of the Waldorf Astoria
to fetch copy about the flower show
at Madison Square Garden.

I quit that job suddenly too.
'You didn't like the export business,'
said Sylvia Cosulich –
I was still seeing her
though her parents didn't approve –
'and you don't want to be a reporter.
What are you going to do?'

In the silence there were sounds
of the traffic down below,
the elevator opening.

               Suddenly
the room seemed far away.
I was looking through a window
at clouds and trees.

And looking down again
to write, as I am now.

Al and Beth

My Uncle Al worked in a drugstore
three blocks above Times Square,
dispensing pills and cosmetics.
All day long crazy people
and thieves came into the store,
but nothing seemed to faze him.

His sister, Beth, was the opposite...
romantic. She used to sing
on ships that sailed from New York
to Central and South America.
When the tourists came trailing back
on board with their maracas,
Beth would be in the Aztec Room
singing 'Smoke Gets in Your Eyes'
and 'I Get a Kick out of You'.

Once when I argued with Al
about something that America
was doing... 'My country
right or wrong,' he told me.
I suppose so, if you've come
from a village in Russia no one
ever heard of, with no drains,
and on saints' days the Cossacks
descend on you with the blessing
of the Church, to beat out your brains.

And when, after a fortnight
being seasick, there's the statue,
and buildings reaching up
to the sky. Streets full of people.
The clang of a bell, someone yelling
as you almost get run over.
More things happening every second
in New York, than Lutsk in a year.

Al lived on Kingston Avenue, Brooklyn,
all of his life, with the wife
his mother had picked out for him.
Beth never married. She was still waiting
for Mr Right.

     Of such is the Kingdom
of Heaven. Say that I sent you.

There You Are

The concierge climbed five flights
to complain. Erich was on the stairs,
just coming up. 'Throw her down,
Vicki,' he shouted, 'I'll catch her!'

There were good times in Paris.
That was before the war,
of course, and La Rafle.

A girl came into the room.
She went over to Erich
and put an arm around him.
'I've done all my homework,
Papa. Can I go now?'

'Lisa is an American girl,'
he said. 'Already she has boyfriends.'

*

La Rafle. I looked it up.
A policeman comes to the door...
'Monsieur, you and Madame
and the children must be packed
and report yourselves to the stadium
tomorrow by seven o'clock.'

So tomorrow, there you are.
And they walk you to the station
and give you to the Germans
with a list of names, and two fingers
to the cap. Signing off.

From there by train to Drancy.
Then Auschwitz, the last stop,
'letzer Termin,' and the gas.

*

It's late, and I'm hurrying
to pack. I have to catch up.
The streets are full of bicycles
going to work. Then I'm running.

And then, with a sense of relief,
I see them up ahead.
There must be thousands moving
like a river through the street.

Some with big suitcases,
looking well dressed and well fed,
others as though they've been living
under a bridge for weeks.

I shout, 'Where are you going?'
'To the station!' they shout back.

Viet-Cong

One moonlit night in Quinhon
they were standing at the window
when she grasped his arm. 'Viet-Cong!'

By moonlight he sees them still,
in black pajamas flitting
like cats from roof to roof.

Honeymoon

Uncle Bob prayed over the groom:
'Let him establish Kingdom principles.'
Aunt Shirley prayed for the bride:
'Father, I pray an anointing on her.'
'Love,' said Reverend Philips,

'is insensitive, love is invalueless.'
He said that we merger together
in holy matrimony,
and the choir burst into song:
'He waits for us, and waits for us.'

*

Every day they went swimming in the pool
and rode the two water scooters.
They rented two deck chairs
and sat on the sand in the sun.
A breeze made the palm leaves whisper.

The sea is green close to shore,
further out it is blue.
The ship standing still on the horizon
makes you think of sailing away
forever with the one you love.

*

Jennifer ordered the roast beef platter.
Mike had the fish cakes.
'I thought you didn't like fish,'
she said. 'Well,' he said, 'I guess you were wrong.'
Tears came to her eyes. The honeymoon was over.

But then they went to their room
and everything was OK.
In the evening they went dancing
and stayed up late on the veranda
looking at the lights and the moon.

*

And you, *hypocrite lecteur*,
what makes you so superior?

An Academic Story

One day during his office hour
a young woman appeared. 'I'm Merridy,'
she said, 'Merridy Johnson.
I'd like you to read my poems.'

He said that he didn't teach writing.
'But couldn't you just look
and tell me, are they any good?'

She was carrying a flat white box.
She removed some tissue paper,
lifted out an album with a red cover,
and handed it to him carefully.

The poems were written in green ink
with flowers and birds in the margins.

She said, 'What do you think?'
He said there were some nice images.
'Where?' she said, and leaned to see.

                    *

His wife didn't go to poetry readings.
He went by himself and sat at the rear.

But this evening he stayed to the end
and went to the reception afterwards
at Professor 'Pat' Melrose's house.

When he arrived the poet was reciting
again, to a circle on the floor.
Merridy patted a place beside her
and he sat.

                    Her eyes were shining.
Poetry gave her goosebumps.
Taking his hand she showed him where.

Melrose was a poet himself.
And there was nothing professorial
about these evenings. They were...bohemian.

Melrose's wife, a little woman
with a face like a rhesus monkey's
went around the room winking and grimacing.
'The pot's in the kitchen, acid's in the study,'
she said with an eldritch laugh.

                    *

He was stoned, and so was she,
going down Spruce Street
with a moon in the redwoods
and San Francisco glittering
on the bay, through the fog.

The poetry was great, she thought.
'As great as Bob Dylan's?'
But irony was wasted on her,
she was innocent. Like her room
with its posters of Joan Baez
and, right on, Bob Dylan.

Her books...*Siddhartha*, Ferlinghetti,
Alan Watts and Suzuki on Zen.
They spoke for her generation
like the *Poems, Sacred and Moral*
of a mid-Victorian girl.

And as softly as saying her prayers
she murmured, 'Let's go to bed.'

                    *

Sam Mendelson was a font of wisdom.
He knew there was going to be an opening
for a medievalist at Ohio,
and who was sleeping with whom.
He said, 'But they don't do it here.
They go to San Francisco.'

The MLA was meeting in San Francisco.
There were sessions he had to go to,
Henry told his wife, Cynthia,
all very boring but unavoidable.
He'd be back in three days.

He and Merridy walked all over.
They ate at Fisherman's Wharf
and rode on a trolley.
They explored Chinatown,
and went dancing at Whisky a Go-Go.
He took her to The Hungry I
and they saw *Doctor Zhivago*.

*

'Cynthia,' he said, 'I'm home!'
No answer. He went upstairs,
unpacked his suitcase, came down,
and was settling in with a scotch
in front of *The Untouchables*
when he had what he could only describe
as a sinking feeling.

He took the stairs two at a time.
No, her dresses were in the closet,
her doodads still on the table.

She came through the door
minutes later. She'd been shopping.
'How was the MLA?'

He gave her a circumstantial account
of the sessions he'd attended
in Yeats and Pound and Eliot.

'I had a vision,' she said.
'I saw you in a room with a woman
as clearly as you're sitting here.'

And he had always thought of her
as a person of limited imagination!

*

He was up for promotion, to associate
with tenure.

           'Melrose is out to get you,'
Sam said. 'Can you think of a reason?'

Henry thought. He shook his head.

'Did you insult Mrs Melrose?'

'I don't recall. I may have.'

At the meeting to decide his fate –
they're supposed to be confidential
but someone always tells –
Melrose spoke.

           His only concern
was in the area of collegiality.

'Associate'…think what that means.
Someone you have to your house,
introduce to your wife…

If the fathers and mothers of the children
to whom we stand *in loco parentis*
were here, they would ask, they would demand to know,
not is he supposed to be clever
and did the *New York Times* or some other publication
give a book a good review,
but is he a moral man?

Henry wasn't promoted and he didn't get tenure.

             *

That was why he was at the MLA.
He was being interviewed at five
by a man from upstate New York.
They had a place for a lost soul
somewhere in the Finger Lakes,
teaching rhetoric.

           'I've never taught it,
but I don't suppose it matters.

I've been speaking it all my life.'
He laughed nervously. 'Shall we have another?'

But I had to go. We were interviewing
on the fourteenth floor.

                    'You're just in time,'
said the Chair. 'Mrs Harris
is going to tell us about her dissertation
on women's writing.'

                    'Ms Harris,'
she said. 'The title is *Theory*
and Praxis in Feminist Criticism.'
In a little while it became obvious
we weren't interviewing her, she was interviewing us.

We used to teach poetry, now it's theory.
There's no longer room in the system
for a mind as romantic as Henry's.

After a Light Snowfall

On a day when snow has fallen
lightly, sprinkling the ground,
and a flock of small birds
are hopping and flying about,
a poem returns to haunt me.

'As you have wasted your life here in this place
You have wasted it in every part of the world.'

I am disturbed by the words
of a man I never knew, who lived
in a country I have never visited.
How is it he knows about me,
and that I have not lived
for the good of others, putting their needs
before my own? That I have not been
a perfect husband and father.
That I have not written a book
that graces every other coffee table,
or made a discovery or invention
that will save lives and relieve human suffering?

How can he say I have wasted my life?
What can he possibly know about me?
And yet I see that he does.

Shoo-Fly Pie

The plain-faced Mennonite woman
with her little white cap
selling cheese and shoo-fly pie...

Existence can be so peaceful –
you only have to be good.
What am I doing here?

A Clearing

I had come to Australia
for ten weeks, as a guest of the state.
My duties were light: to confer
with students. They didn't want to –
they came once or twice, that was all.

One night someone knocked: a student
with some poems she'd like me to see.
The next day I observed her
in the dining room, and went over.
'I liked' I began to say…
She lifted her hands, imploring me
not to speak. All around her
they were talking about the usual subjects,
motorbikes and football.
If it got around that she wrote poems…

At night I would sit in my room
reading, keeping a journal,
and, with the aid of a map,
trying to learn the positions
of the southern constellations.
I'd look at them on the map,
then go outside and try to find them
in the sky before I forgot.

I had recently been divorced
and was starting a new life,
as they say. The world lies before you,
where to live and what to be.
A fireman? An explorer?
An astronaut? Then you look in the mirror.
It was night sweats. Listening
to an echo of the end.

*

Roger had a live-in girlfriend.
They asked if I'd like to go with them
to a party and sleep over.

He drove. I looked at the gum trees.
Not the Outback, but country...
cattle and kangaroos,
and flies, getting in your eyes,
ears, nose, and mouth.
Once, talking to a sheepherder,
I watched a fly crawl over his face
from his eye to his mouth,
and start walking back
before he brushed it off.
They learn to put up with nature
and not make a fuss like us.

We arrived. I was introduced,
and they made up a bed for me
on the porch at the back.
Then the party began to arrive:
Australians, lean and athletic.
They put a tape on the stereo,
turned it up full blast,
and danced, or stood and shouted
to each other above to noise.

I danced with two or three women
and tried shouting. Then I went
and sat on the bed on the porch.
There was nowhere to go, no door
I could close to shut out the noise.

*

So I went for a walk
in the dark, away from the sound.
There were gum trees, wind rustling
the leaves. Or was it snakes?

There are several venomous kinds.
The taipan. There's a story
about a child who was sitting
on a log and fell backward
onto a taipan. It struck him
twenty-three times.

There's the tiger snake and the brown.
When they have finished telling you
about snakes, they start on spiders.

You don't need these – you have only to walk
into the bush. There are stories
about campers who did, and were lost
and never seen again.

All this was on my mind.
I stepped carefully, keeping the lights
of the house behind me in sight.
And when I saw a clearing
in the trees, I walked to it.

                            *

I stood in the middle of the clearing
looking at the sky. It was glittering
with unknown constellations.
Everything I had ever known
seemed to have disappeared.
And who was I, standing there
in the middle of Australia
at night? I had ceased to exist.
There was only whatever it was
that was looking at the sky
and listening to the wind.

After a while I broke away
and went back to the lights and the party.
A month later I left Australia.

But ever since, to this day,
there has been a place in my mind,
a clearing in the shadows,
and above it, stars and constellations
so bright and thick they seem to rustle.
And beyond them... infinite space,
eternity, you name it.

There's nothing that stands between me
and it, whatever it is.

The Long Afternoon

Behind the glass door
stands a *babushka*,
a grandmother doll.
It unscrews. There's another
inside, a size smaller,
that unscrews, and so on.

A pipe called a *hookah*
with a malachite bowl...

The gramophone wheezes,
scratches, and speaks:
'Say It With Music.'
White flannels and knees
intently two-stepping
step out on the floor.

At four there's a breeze.
The bamboo trunks creak
and talk in the lane.
A house lizard hops
from the vine to the rail...
cocks his head at me.

'Remember?' he croaks.
Dear brother, I do!

The Listeners

I walked down the street
to the harbor, by gardens
with tattered leaves and weeds,
and through an open gate.

The red roof of the house
had lost its tiles in patches,
and the windows had no glass.
A woman stood in a window

looking down. 'I used to live here,'
I shouted. 'Is it all right
if I just look around?'

        *

A man with dreadlocks sat
on his heels, doing something
to a pot. A child stood by him.
I walked down to the shore.

A man came towards me.
His name was Rohan Moore.
Was I the owner, he asked.
No, I said, and heard

the appreciative murmur
of those who were listening
to my life as to a play.

        *

Rohan Moore led the way
into the house. It was dark.
The wall was unpainted,
the railing rough to the hand.

A family lived in the room...
it seemed, in every corner,
and still there was a space
where a bed once stood, by the wall,

with a table, glass and spoon.
My father, looking small,
spoke again the last few words.

     *

People were gathering
from every part of the house,
a dozen where four used to be.
They stood and stared silently.

I shook the hand of my guide,
now my friend. And another's.
'You can come and live here,
if you want,' Rohan said.

There were sounds of laughter,
chairs pushed back, and voices
in the distance, going away.

The Floor Lamp

He threw his belongings
in one of the matching suitcases.
And the floor lamp was his.

He took a taxi to the station.
The lamp was awkward to carry.
The shade tilted like a hat.

Suppose he just left it...
He could see it on the platform,
waiting for him to come back.

The early commuters
would step around it.
Later when everyone was hurrying

it would fall with a crack.
He picked up the floor lamp,
and the suitcase, and turned back.

A Walk with Bashō

Old boards by the sea
when the tide runs around them
still yearn to sail free.

The moon bright and round
troubles my heart. The old pond
frog-jumping-in sound.

Confessions of a Professor of English

It was beautiful in Berkeley
looking across the bay
at the lights of San Francisco.

A man from one of the oldest families,
who had lived in the Bay Area
all his life, told me, 'I moved once,
to Oakland. But I moved back.
San Francisco is where it's at.'
He was writing a book, *Queen City
of the Pacific*. 'How do you like it?
I mean as a title?' I said
I liked it. I really did. It had a ring.

One day, during my office hour
I was reading *The Faerie Queene*,
which I detested but was required
to teach, when a pair of heels
came running down the corridor.
A young woman in a miniskirt
went sobbing by my door,
and she shouted, 'Oh my God!'
People came out of their offices.
Whittaker who was in the 18th century
put out his head. 'What was that?'
'I don't know,' I said. 'Search me.'

One day Jim Anderson was shot
by a deranged former student
who walked in with a shotgun.
Jim lived, but the graduate student
who was with him, jumped up
and got the other barrel in his back,
and died on the spot.

I mention these things only because
they were so unusual. Otherwise
time just seemed to go by.

But then there was the Free Speech Movement.
While trying to teach *The Faerie Queene*
you heard the loudspeakers in the Plaza...
Goldberg, Aptheker, Mario Savio.
The students sat in Sproul Hall.
Joan Baez arrived, and led the way,
singing, 'We Shall Overcome.'
The students lay down and were carried
by policemen, and put in paddy wagons.

I left in '67, and so missed
the People's Park, helicopters spraying
students and faculty alike with tear gas.
All of that.

What a strange thing it was
to be a professor of English!
Once at a faculty meeting I heard
a professor who shall be nameless
say that D.H. Lawrence was
'an uneducated man'.
Not that I like D.H. Lawrence...
Like the author of *The Faerie Queene*
he's one of the bastards I'm glad
I shall never have to meet.
Once he threw a little dog he had,
I think its name was Bibbles,
against a rock.
But 'uneducated'? Oh my god!

I do remember the faces
of some students. The happy few.
In a few years, I told them,
there'll be no more Departments
of English. Not to worry,
it will be like the Middle Ages:
enclaves of those who can read.
And when there's a famine or plague
the people will take them out and kill them.
But poetry won't die,
for there'll always be a poet.

They were listening intently,
except for the two in the back.
A colleague told me once,
'I heard some students talking about you.
One said, 'I like to hear him rave.' ''

A Farewell to His Muse

The floorboards creak
and I lie thinking.
Timor mortis **non** *conturbat me.*
The idea of dying
doesn't frighten me a bit,
nor the bad road to it,
sans eyes, sans teeth....

But the muse has left my bed,
having removed her things
on the sly, thinking
I don't notice, the bitch!
Go on, why don't you
just say it, 'I don't love you.'
Leave! Get the hell out!
I don't want to know who with.

Some talentless creep
from a Creative Writing
and Poetry Business School.
Get on line – *vita brevis* –
prostrate yourself,
crawl on hands and knees,
and kiss her *ars longa.*

He's got it all worked out:
two years to a Guggenheim,
followed by the reward
of genius, a MacArthur;
in ten, with the assistance
of friends, the Pulitzer.
Finally to sit in state
in the National Academy
and Institute of Conniving...

*

Well, easy come,
easy go. And it's been fun.
Farewell the something something
that make ambition virtue.

There was a time I could quote
the Bard by the yard,
but I had to give it up.
There is nothing you can learn
from the English, except
how to talk like a gentleman
with your nose in the air
and marbles in your mouth.

In fact, there was nothing
I could learn from anyone.
All you really know is given
at moments when you're seeing
and listening.

                Being in love
is a great help.

Oh yes, but keep a dog.

A Shearling Coat

Alexander Ortiz and Arlyne Gonzales
were walking home from a movie.

A car drew up, and two men
got out. One had a gun, the other

tugged at her shearling coat.
'Don't hurt her,' Ortiz said, 'she's pregnant.'

The gunman shot him twice,
in the chest and throat.

'What you do that for?' said the other.
'C'mon, c'mon, get the jacket,'

the gunman said, and they left,
with a parting shot at Gonzales.

She had thrown herself down
on top of the dying man.

And I shall be wanting to be rid
of this thing to the end of my days.

Variations on a Theme by Shostakovich

Galich…the name leapt at me
from a shelf. It's a sign,
I said to myself.
But his real name was Ginzburg.

It's not such a good idea
to be a Jew in Russia.
He took the name of a teacher
of the great poet Pushkin.

For he too was a poet,
though mainly he wrote plays,
about mixups, misunderstandings,
romance…that kind of thing.

They were enormously successful.
Moreover, he was handsome
and charming. 'The most popular man
in Russia,' somebody said.

*

These were the years when Stalin
was shunting people off
to Siberia, where they died.
The time of Virta's 'no conflict theory'…
There could be no conflict in plays
written in the Soviet Union:
there was only a struggle
between the 'good' and the 'better.'

Galich titled one of his plays
Moscow Does Not Believe in Tears.

But let him tell it himself:
'Many times, many ways, we played silent parts,
and our silence meant "yes" and not "no".'

*

Josef Stalin died at last,
but his pall-bearers clung
to power, like lice in a coat.

Galich sang openly
of the lies and injustices
he saw in the life around him.

He joined the Orthodox Church.
A 'Committee for Human Rights'!
Sasha, where are you going?

He signed an open letter
calling for amnesty
for all political prisoners.

He called for repeal of the law
that prohibited Jews from emigrating.
Ginzburg, you'd better look out!

*

To the meeting of the Writers' Union
to discuss Galich's behavior
came a man named Arbuzov.

He had it in for Galich.
The members of a collective
had written a play... Arbuzov
published it under his name.
Galich spoke of this with contempt.

The meeting of the tribunal
gave Arbuzov his chance.
He shed tears... he was shaken,
he said, at having to bear witness
to the depths to which the man had sunk.

The meeting became a celebration
of Arbuzov, and Galich was expelled,
cast out of the Writers' Union.
He would not be permitted
to publish his work from now on.

And then he was banned
by the Litfond, the body
that gave financial aid to writers.

                    *

At the corner of Sadovaya Street
Galich ran into three men
who were out for a good time.
They knocked off his hat.

'You old *git*,' they said,
'when are you going to leave the country?'
'What do you mean?'
he stammered. 'This is my home.'

But he and his wife were starving.
After several applications
they had a permit to leave...
at once, within twenty-four hours.

They did, and were made welcome
in Norway. Then they traveled
through Europe, Galich performing
his songs to the guitar.

Finally they made their home in Paris.

                    *

He was doing something with a wire
and the tape recorder.

He put the plug in a socket
and saw the domes of Moscow

shining like peeled onions,
pffi! and he was dead.

'Isn't that your hat?'
Pushkin said. He picked it up,

brushed it with his sleeve,
and put it on Galich's head.

The Owner of the House

The movers came, and took
her bed, table, everything,
until the house was empty.

She was walking on a road
at night, in a dark dress,
and so she was hit.

A driver who had seen it
said that he thought someone
threw a doll up in the air.

          *

I found some smaller things
that had been overlooked.
A fish made of wood.

A bell, perhaps for calling
a cat. Every night
one comes around and mourns.

A hidden drawer with thread
and needle, thimble, things
as hidden as a heart.

          *

She let the house run down,
the garden be overgrown,
lost in her arcane studies.

They had to do with the eye
of a fish that she had found
somewhere in Mexico.

A neighbor disconnected
the refrigerator, but did not
think to empty it. Fishes stink.

          *

I open the door of a cabinet
and forget to close it again –
whack! The side of my head.

'Just to remind you,'
she whispers, 'it's my house.'
The carpenters are hard at work –

I need more space. She stands
watching a while, and leaves.
She'll have the run of it still.

Struggling Times

One hour they lay buried beneath the ruins of that hall;
But as the stars rise from the salt lake they arise in pain,
In troubled mists o'erclouded by the terrors of struggling times.

WILLIAM BLAKE, 'Europe, A Prophecy'

1

We have lost our investments.
The pillars of the kingdom are broken.
This morning's *New York Times*

reports that the ongoing
criminal investigation
is expanding to the banks

that have flown to Bermuda.
Once you could get a basket
of worms and go fishing,

but the rivers too are polluted.
So we shall stay at home
and on Sunday go to church

and hear the priest, who is young
and recently married, preach
on sin and love, and the difference.

2

At the meeting of the Senate
Judiciary Committee
Mr Kilov, a biologist,

said that the treaties were only paper,
and inspections were useless.
A weapon of mass destruction

could be made by a few professionals,
biologists and chemists, working
in a small, hidden space.

3

You have to be careful
what you hear or see.
In Afghanistan I saw

the man and the woman
who were caught in adultery
buried up to their heads.

Their children were brought
and told to throw stones.
I can still see the heads

twisting on the ground.
The poor devil in *Papillon*
with his head in the guillotine...

but Goya's half-buried dog
looking up at the sky
I think was the worst of all.

Suddenly

The truck came at me,
I swerved
but I got a dent.

The car insurance woman
informs me that my policy
has been cancelled.

I say, 'You can't do that.'
She gives me a little smile
and goes back to her nails.

Lately have you noticed
how aggressively people drive?
A *whoosh!* and whatever.

Some people are suddenly
very rich, and as many
suddenly very poor.

As for the war, don't get me started.
We were too busy watching
the ball game to see

that the things we care about
are suddenly disappearing,
and that they always were.

A New Year's Child

He wants me to carry him.
It's an order, and I obey.

Though it isn't easy...
he twists and turns in my arms,

he wants to see everything
in the world all at once.

Where are his parents?
The man and the woman

talking so seriously...
The man leans over and gives her

a kiss on the cheek.
The child looks at me

as if to say, 'Did you see that?'
and he laughs.

I could carry this child
forever, he feels so light.

A Spot on the Kitchen Floor

A spot was moving slowly
across the kitchen floor.

I placed a card in front of it.
The bug, for such it was,

climbed on, and continued
to move...without legs

apparently, like a toy.
I tilted the card,

and the bug went wild,
running in a circle,

and back to the door,
where it vanished.

There's nothing much doing
here. We might have talked.

An Impasse

Jacques writes from Paris,
'What are the latest news?'

I have told him, time
and time again, 'What are'

is not English, 'news'
is not plural, 'news'

is a singular term, as in 'The news is good.'

He replies, 'Though "The news"
may be singular in America,

it is not so in France.
Les nouvelles is a plural term.

To say, "The news is good"
in France would be bad grammar,

and absurd, which is worse.
On the other hand, "What are

the news?" makes perfect sense.'

My Life the Movie

His is nattily dressed
like a French officer,
in a uniform with boots.

A woman with long black hair
comes in. She looks distracted.
She runs toward him,

and clasps him in her arms.
He stands stock still,
and the director shouts, 'Cut!'

                    *

A conference is in progress.
An older man with gray hair,
the CEO, is in charge.

'You took your time getting here,'
says one of the conferees,
and laughs. He's no friend of mine.

But the CEO smiles,
and the faces turned to me
at the long table are smiling.

                    *

I have ideas
that seem so real
that the characters,

who I have never seen,
must be alive somewhere.
If I went there, they would be:

the unmoving Frenchman,
the beautiful, distracted girl,
the smiling, gray-haired CEO.

Consolations

Dickinson had a cockatoo
she called Semiramis
and loved dearly.

Whitman was a trencherman,
his favorite dish
a mulligan stew.

Frost went for long walks.
Eliot played croquet.
Pound took fencing lessons.

There is a snapshot of Yeats
with a woman in a garden,
naked to the waist and smiling.

Auden, when he was old,
counted the sheets of toilet paper
that a visitor used.

Mr and Mrs Yeats

'The common condition
of our life,' Yeats said,
'is hatred.'

You might think as he did
if you loved a woman
who never would love you,
an angry, shouting woman,
a woman like Maud Gonne.

And if instead of love
you had 'theatre business',
and your better moments
were at the club, 'exchanging
polite meaningless words'.

But then, suppose you met
a women, oddly named,
who had a kinder face.
George helped him understand
the phases of the moon.

She talked to the great dead
in automatic writing.
Yeats and his wife together
went up a winding stair
that leads...I don't know where.

(It wasn't a religion,
Yeats despised religion.)
The point is, he discovered
the common life of man
and woman could be kind.

And if it wasn't love,
as love is in the movies,
they didn't seem to mind.

The Glass Eel Gatherer

We were watching the team
at practice – counting to ten,
running at each other,
colliding in helmets,
and falling down again.

Was she a fan?

Hardly, she said.
She was taking a break
from her job, biology,
i.e., glass eels.

They were transparent.
She was doing research,
counting and measuring. Actually
Europeans consider them
a delicacy.

'Europeans!' I snorted,
and she laughed.

I was considering her.
But she had a friend…
she mentioned him twice.
So that was that. She returned
to the country of Might Have Been.

But whenever I'm feeling
out of sorts for some reason…
a serial murderer
has been given a parole
for good behavior.
Or the generals are sure
they have everything in hand.

Or the fact that nobody
in the world gives a damn
for anything I think or do…
Will there still be Medicare

when I am old? Will I be able
to lean over and tie my shoes?

I see myself in one room
with all my books, and no one
to talk to but Proust, and he's dead.

At such times I think about her,
my lovely glass eel gatherer.
She is down by the water,
in her waders and her shorts,
and a shirt that is wet
and transparent.

She is standing perfectly still,
looking down at the water.
Then she stoops and carefully
stands up with something,
a vessel, in her hands,
and brings it, and shows me
glass eels.

Jabez

Cloaked reports of shotguns…
all the fathers are out,

birds flying over.
I'm tugging at the trigger

of the little shotgun
Rosalind never used,

but it doesn't move.
Baldpate and Whitewing

are flying past.
'Yuh got de savety on,'

Jabez says, and shows me.
I'm too tired to walk,

so Jabez carries me
all the way back.

I don't say thank you
to Jabez. He's my friend.

Piano Rolls

Tranströmer had a stroke.
His right arm was useless

and he struggled for words.
We tried to understand.

He stood up suddenly,
went over to the piano,

and played for his guests
music for the left hand.

*

The Mafia killed his father
for some reason – Cosa Nostra.

Then offered his mother
money. She walked away.

He was too young
to kill them, so he smiles.

I have seen him at work,
hammering and twisting metal.

*

Life will soon be over,
you think.

No sooner do you
think so, than

she comes bustling in
with a pretty knee

and a teapot, humming
'Amazing Grace'.

*

Buster was my dog.
They sent me to boarding school.

When I came back he was gone.
They never told me why.

They must have got rid of him.
This is the worst thing

that ever happened to me.
It was worse than the war.

                    *

She died in her sleep,
an age of voyages

in interstellar space,
world changing policies,

a war fought over oil.
But nothing changes

the color of her eyes,
the corner of a smile.

Aston and Rosalind

Buying a House

We were living in a house
my father was thinking of buying.
A door suddenly opened
and who should come in
but my mother, Rosalind.
She was holding a revolver.
'Now Rosalind,' he said.
He walked across the room
and took the gun from her hand.
She fell to the floor,
foaming at the mouth.
I was seven years old.
I thought she was mad.

Cosmetics

She flew to New York.
There was an opening
for cosmetics in Venezuela.
Helena Rubinstein gave her
a contract, then tried to break it.
She got a good lawyer and beat them.

She married a…Renato
who was good-looking,
and bought a house in Viareggio.
Not a house, a palazzo.
They called it Villa Rosalinda.

Not bad for a girl who was born
in Lutsk!

On the boat that was bringing her
to America she gave her last
kopec for a bowl of soup
and saved her sister's life.

On the Jitney

Trilling gives me a look
of mild exasperation.

Then I wake up. It's Monday.
I am on the Jitney.
Thank God I didn't miss it.
If I did what would I find to eat?
Pickles would hardly do it.

I have an exciting life.
Actually I do, with all my narrow
escapes. Taking books back to
the library before they are overdue
and I'm fined thirty or even sixty cents.

Another thing would be driving.
But I don't want to
talk about that.

Most of the people driving
are insane, filled with rage.
How did that start? Not just the men
but women too.
God help you if you get in the way.

So I gave up driving.
How do I get around?
I have some friends,
and the Jitney.

There is one thing I don't
like to think too much about.
The people on the Jitney
are old, and getting older.

They are nearly all women.
The women talk and laugh,
they seem to be enjoying the ride.

There are one or two men.
They bury themselves in the news,
and say goodbye. That is all.

Louis Simpson was born in Jamaica in 1923, the son of a lawyer of Scottish descent and a Russian mother. Educated at Munro College (Jamaica) and at Columbia University, New York, where he received his doctorate, he taught at Columbia, the University of California at Berkeley, and at the State University of New York at Stony Brook. He has published 19 books of poetry, most recently, *The Owner of the House: New Collected Poems 1940–2001* (BOA Editions, USA, 2003), which was shortlisted for the Griffin Prize and was a finalist for the National Book Award in Poetry; his most recent new collection, *Struggling Times* (BOA Editions, USA, 2009); and *Voices in the Distance: Selected Poems* (Bloodaxe Books, 2010), his first UK selected poems since *People Live Here: Selected Poems 1949–1983* (BOA Editions, USA, 1983; Secker & Warburg, UK, 1985). He has received the Rome Fellowship of the American Academy of Arts and Letters, a Hudson Review fellowship, Guggenheim Foundation fellowships, and the Pulitzer Prize. Simpson lives in Stony Brook, Long Island, New York.